The Heart of Esthetics

Creating Loyal Clients &
Achieving Financial Success

DIANE BUCCOLA

DEDICATION

This book is dedicated to all the hard-working Professional Estheticians who share my passion for the esthetics business and continually put in the effort to raise the standards of this career that we love.

CONTENTS

ACKNOWLEDGMENTS

Many thanks to the members of SpaBizBoard who have been my biggest source of inspiration since 2006. I would also like to acknowledge Susanne Warfield and NCEA for all that you do to preserve and protect our beloved esthetics careers. And to my followers at Happy Esthetician, thank you so much for your support over the years.

1 A NOTE FROM DIANE

Throughout this book, I will give you bits of background about various parts of my career and my life that eventually shaped who I became as an Esthetician, spa owner, and author of The Heart of Esthetics. I have made plenty of mistakes, but by a huge margin, I have been blessed. I have had so many wonderful mentors throughout my career who guided me along the way to my success. My wish for you is that my lessons, and this book, will help you sidestep any bumps in the road that you may encounter and will guide you along the path as you follow your own esthetics journey.

WHY I WROTE THIS BOOK

As of this writing, I have been an esthetician for 22 years. I have worn a lot of hats in this business, but I have never been as excited and passionate about anything related to the spa business as I am about this book. However, this book is not about me. It's about you -- who you are, and who you want to be -- in your esthetics career.

In this book, I talk a lot about passion. Esthetics is my passion. I am fascinated with the "psychology" of the esthetics business, such as what makes a consumer choose one spa or Esthetician over another, or what compels one client to buy and another to walk away.

There is a science and a simple formula for success in the esthetics business, and you are about to find out what it is.

I wrote The Heart of Esthetics book because it is my personal belief that Estheticians serve a higher purpose that goes well beyond skin care. A really good Esthetician can actually change a client's life. I wrote this book because it brought me joy, and if reading this book helps you in some way, my heart is happy.

I believe that as Estheticians, we are all in this together. And I believe that we are only as strong as our weakest link. Because of that, I have spent many years trying to raise the standards of this career that I love with a goal to ensure that the field of esthetics remains strong and viable.

SpaBizBoard

One of my early efforts was the creation of SpaBizBoard which I launched in 2006. SpaBizBoard was the first private members-only online community for spa professionals. Back then, new Estheticians were coming out of their esthetics program with nobody to talk to, no one to bounce ideas off, nobody to answer questions…with the exception of their fellow esthetics school students whose education was at the same newbie level as their own.

During SpaBizBoard's 11-year run, I had a front row seat to the struggles and successes of Estheticians from all over the USA, Canada and Europe. Our members were made up of spa owners, Solo Estheticians, esthetics instructors, manufacturers of professional skin care products and equipment, trainers, authors…the list goes on and on.

SpaBizBoard members felt safe to speak openly in our community because not only was the site off limits to the public, but because I personally verified every person who requested membership. Needless to say, I learned a lot during that time.

SpaBizBoard had a huge impact on who I became as an Esthetician, then speaker, consultant and author, which eventually led me to write The Heart of Esthetics book.

Because of my unique position as the owner of SpaBizBoard, I was aware, on a 24/7 basis, of the struggles that Estheticians and spas often endured. I knew what the obstacles were, and I knew how to eliminate them. I learned the wrong turns and I could see the right turns. I witnessed the paths that led them to struggle, and I watched the paths that ultimately led them to success.

I retired SpaBizBoard at the end of 2017 simply because 11 years of checking Esthetician licenses from all over the country finally wore me out. However, the friends I made during those years remain very strong, and I know those friendships will last forever.

Know your Sources

I also am aware of the massive amount of bad advice that is regularly dispensed from "consultants" who are not actively involved in the esthetics business, as well as volumes of misinformation found on social media. You see, our business is very different from all the rest. Ours is intimate, it is personal, and it is ever evolving. This means that if an advisor is not currently hands-on in the treatment room, that advisor may not be the best qualified to advise us.

To maintain the integrity that I believe is crucial for the success of Estheticians, you will never see me making our trade secrets accessible for public consumption on social media. For example, I don't belong to any Facebook esthetics groups that I don't own and manage myself. Nor will you find me uploading YouTube videos which contain secrets from the treatment room. I will only share my knowledge with Professional Estheticians.

So ladies and gentlemen, throughout this book I will repeat these words frequently: "Know your sources." It is just so important! This applies to any advice you are being given, by anyone, whether it is online, at a trade show, or from a consultant.

For example, if someone is offering advice about a marketing idea to bring in new clients, ask questions such as "Did you actually try this in your esthetics business? How well did it work? By what method were you able to track how many people responded? Was it highly profitable for you? How many people scheduled appointments as a direct result of that specific marketing strategy?"

Keep in mind that you may not always be getting the full story from people on social media. In fact, many Estheticians are working very hard to get attention so their goal is more along the lines of: "Please look at me!!" For which I am thinking, "How about instead of looking for attention, you put that time and effort into serving your clients?"

In my experience, I know these two things to be true:

1. Those on social media who brag about their success probably are not as successful as they would like others to believe.
2. Those who are really are successful probably are not going to brag on social media about their success.

EXTRAS

You will find scattered throughout this book little extras called "Behind the Scenes" which are scenarios that I have encountered and lessons I have learned while working as a consultant. Some of those include "Notes for Spa Owners" which is offered for those of you who have employees.

I have also included a handful of what I am calling "Personal Development Tools" which are exercises to help you find clarity. And here is the first one:

PERSONAL DEVELOPMENT TOOL #1
Navigating Fear

We can't talk about creating a successful esthetics business (or any other business, for that matter) without first discussing fear. Here's the thing about fear: The real reason we don't move creatively ahead is always and only fear.

And how do you know fear is the obstacle? Because fear will stop you. Remember this: Things do not have to be perfect. They just have to get done. You will reach your version of perfection someday, but only if you begin…and then keep moving forward through the fear.

Giving up on a goal because of a setback
is like slashing your other three tires because you got a flat.

Here is something I am borrowing from the author Elizabeth Gilbert. You probably know her from the book and movie "Eat Pray Love." Below is her explanation regarding how she navigates the path of fear. (She used an expletive, which I have edited…but I'm sure you get the gist). When you run up against a fearful moment or situation, apply her advice to fit your specific situation:

Sh*t Sandwiches:

> Finding your true purpose is really just deciding which sh*t sandwich you're in for. The question is <u>not</u> "What do I love?" The question is "What do I love so much that I don't mind eating the sh*t sandwich that comes along with that thing?"

> For example, as a successful writer, getting a bad review in a prominent newspaper, or an awful comment on social media (sh*t sandwiches), do I still want to do this thing? YES.

> If the first time I encounter a sh*t sandwich and I say, "This isn't worth it"…then this is not the thing I should be doing.

> If you go into this thing thinking, "If I follow my bliss, and I live my dream, and I stand in my truth, then everything will be great," that doesn't necessarily mean everything will actually be great. It just means at the end of the day when you check in with yourself, you ask yourself, "Is this still better

than not doing it?" And if the answer is, "YES, this thing is still better than not doing it," then you are on the right path.

And suddenly you know it's time to start something new...
and trust the magic of beginnings.
~Meister Eckhart

So my fellow Estheticians, spa owners, and esthetics students: Whether you are a seasoned Esthetician who is suffering from a bit of burnout, or you are a new Esthetician who is ready to jumpstart your career, reading The Heart of Esthetics book is definitely a big first step on the right path. I named this book "The **Heart** of Esthetics" for a very important reason...and you are about to find out what that reason is.

Here we go!

Diane

2 THE LIVES OF WOMEN

You may not yet realize it, but as an Esthetician, you are part of something much bigger than just your esthetics skills. That's because our business is not *really* about facials and products. Those are simply tools that we use in our work. Success in the esthetics business is built on relationships.

The bond you develop with your clients -- while based upon the skin care services you provide -- has many other components that are not related to the client's skin. Therefore, even if you get the skin care element of your work right, it does not guarantee that you won't lose a client for other reasons And when that happens, odds are that you will never figure out why. On the other hand, when you understand your clients and are able to master the tools you will learn in this book, you are on your way to becoming a rock star Esthetician.

THE BAROMETER OF SUCCESS
IN THE ESTHETICS BUSINESS

Of course, we love our male clients. I certainly do! And fortunately for us, men's interest in skin care is increasing exponentially. However, that has not changed the fact (so far) that the barometer of success in the esthetics business is <u>the lives of women</u>.

What this means for Estheticians is that even if you have the finest esthetics skills, the highest-quality professional skin care products, a lovely facility, and access to many wonderful clients, if you don't understand the mindset of your clients (and potential clients), your path to success could be a little bumpy. This of course includes our male clients, female clients, and everything in between, however, in this section we are focusing on the lives of women.

Notes from Your Fairy Godmother

Below is an excerpt from my book "Notes from Your Fairy Godmother." The book is not about esthetics, but there is one section about "beauty" that applies to Estheticians and their clients.

I am including this information here to give you a glimpse into what is being subliminally absorbed into the minds of women. Advertisers target women specifically by focusing on the TV channels and other media that are primarily viewed by a female audience. I researched this phenomena in 2017 while I was writing "Notes from Your Fairy Godmother."

My research included noting the ads that played during movies and other content on channels geared toward women such as Hallmark, Bravo, etc. The result was astonishing. Whether a woman is aware of it or not, this marketing has an effect on her…and therefore an effect on our role as her Esthetician.

Here is the excerpt from my book which is the direct result of my research on this topic:

> "Women are regularly exposed to ad campaigns suggesting that we should lose weight, exercise more, eat this, don't eat that. There are age-shaming ads implying that we need to fix something. We are encouraged to lift, tuck, flatten, lose, add, remove, install, inject, cut, dye, lengthen, shorten, ingest a supplement, sign up for a program, or model ourselves after celebrities.

As a result of this marketing strategy, self-image takes up a lot of space in the brains of many women. It clutters our mind to the point that we are unable to appreciate our own beauty as we continue to evolve throughout our lives. We are typically our own worst critic, however our criticisms are not based upon who we really are, but rather who we think we should be according to input from external sources. What woman hasn't at one time or another said to herself (or to others), "I hate my _____" (arms, legs…fill in the blank)?

We weren't born this way, but we have unintentionally picked up this burden and we carry it with us every day of our lives. If we could eliminate the self-critical thinking, can you imagine all the extra space we'd have in our brains to think about other, more pleasant things? If only we could enlighten girls about this at a younger age, what a wonderful life experience they would have!

By no means do I mean to imply that women should avoid all anti-aging efforts, because I really don't feel that way. Certainly, if something makes you feel good, do it. But the methods offered for improvement are becoming further invasive and frighteningly extreme. Many great ideas come from fashion and beauty resources, of course, but we've got to find a way to keep everything in perspective and not abandon our spirit while chasing physical perfection. *(Excerpted from "Notes from Your Fairy Godmother" by Diane Buccola.)*

As Estheticians, this is one of the reasons we must keep in mind the very personal and somewhat intimate relationship we have with our clients. And by "personal" and "intimate," I am referring to the fact that when a new client enters our treatment room, she is asked to remove most of her clothing, put on a facial wrap, and crawl into something that looks a lot like a bed. Then all of her makeup is removed by a person she may have just met for the first time, who then places a bright magnifying lamp directly over her face.

Especially for first-timers, this can be a distressing -- or at the very least, unpleasant experience. No wonder some women are hesitant to come to an Esthetician for a facial. For those women, the easier solution is to buy products online, at a department store, or from an MLM salesperson.

If you could put yourself into the shoes of this new client even for a moment, you would be able to understand that the connection she has with us, as well as the comfort she feels while in our space, begins very quickly and runs very deep. This is why our Esthetician license, our continuing esthetics education, and our participation at professional esthetics trade show is essential to a strong bond with our clients.

(Es-the-tish-uhn) n.

A person skilled in the art of skin care treatments; facials, waxing; well-versed in the subject of skin care and maintenance.

A smart individual who has contracted a case of skin health sense and is determined to spread the condition.

Synonyms: Aesthetician, skin care goddess, facial diva, sunscreen queen, friend, secret-keeper, holder of the key to the Fountain of Youth.

Common tools: Fan brush, steamer, extractor, tweezers, waxing sticks, magic wrinkle eraser.

MY STORY

It's not that my esthetics journey is particularly special. I've certainly made plenty of mistakes, but I have also enjoyed great success. Through it all, I have learned a lot, and the purpose of sharing these details here with you is to offer ideas that may be of help as you follow your own esthetics journey.

"My dream was not specifically to become an Esthetician, however I found my niche in esthetics."
~Diane Buccola

My "A-ha" Moments

My route to becoming an Esthetician was a bit convoluted. Of all the things I thought I wanted to be when I grew up, Esthetician was not one of them (possibly because that title did not exist back then). The majority of my adult years were spent in the field of law: Law Office Manager, Court Reporter and wife of a trial lawyer. Needless to say, facials and bikini waxing were definitely not on my radar.

During my many years as a Court Reporter, I worked as an Independent Contractor and later I opened my own Court Reporting firm. As my business grew, I hired employees and other Independent Contractors. However, when I got married and started a family, I took a few years off, fully intending to go back to my court reporting career that I had worked so hard to create. However, I quickly realized that the inflexibility and stress of a busy Court Reporter was not conducive to a happy family life. That's when I decided to follow a long-held dream which was to open a wellness center for women.

The reason a women's wellness center was in the back of my mind goes way back to my younger days. My family owned three upscale women's clothing stores (and one children's store) for over 25 years. I began working at one of the women's clothing stores when I was around 11 years old doing simple things like wrapping presents, making bows, unpacking shipments of clothing, and steaming. Lots and lots of steaming. Throughout the years, I worked my way up through the ranks to sales associate, and eventually I left the family business and went off to do my own thing.

THE ANNUAL FASHION SHOW

My family's stores held fashion shows for women throughout the year. Most were smaller venues, like restaurants, malls, county fairs. Attendance was free at these events. I modeled in these shows beginning when I was in about 2nd grade, modeling apparel from our children's store, and into my early 20's. I mention this because it was at these shows that I began to be exposed to the perception many women have about themselves.

Once a year, we held a much anticipated and very well-attended fashion show which was held in a large venue such as a convention center. Other local businesses were brought in to assist with various aspects of this annual event. I modeled in these shows too and at this time in my life, I also taught aerobics a couple nights a week at a local health club. The health club was one of the businesses we partnered with for the annual fashion show.

Makeover Mommies. Months before the annual fashion show, we put out a call for females who wanted a complete makeover, which back then simply involved hair, makeup and clothing style (unlike today's version of a "Mommy Makeover" which typically involves surgery).

The applications came in like crazy, and I began to notice a thread of commonality among the women who were applying. They were young mothers, and in their applications they noted that they just didn't feel pretty. They felt overweight, they had lost their mojo, and they didn't feel good about themselves.

I was barely in my 20s back then, so I wasn't a mother and didn't understand any of that personally, but even then, I noticed this obvious pattern. In retrospect, I really think that experience is what planted the seed that eventually grew into "Diane Buccola, Esthetician."

The lucky participants were given a 6-week makeover which included nutrition and fitness classes at the health club where I worked. The women were sent to a hair salon where they were treated to a complete consultation and a hair makeover. The final element of their makeover was a makeup consultation and update by a professional makeup artist.

Backstage on the day of the annual fashion show, these beautiful ladies were treated to a full day of style as they prepared to make their runway debut. Their makeup was professionally applied, their hair was professionally styled, they put on their fashion show clothing which had been previously selected and fitted to them. At the appointed time, they strode down the catwalk as their new fabulously fit, healthy, and stylish selves.

For all the years I was part of the annual fashion show, I had the privilege of seeing so many women transform from no mojo to mucho mojo! They went from not feeling good about themselves to being excited to show themselves off as they practically floated out on that stage. I swear, there was an actual light that shone from them when they walked the runway. It was amazing to see!

That experience stuck with me throughout all the years that followed. And that is where my desire to help women feel better about themselves came from. I wanted to be part of that. And as an Esthetician, I have been. For over two decades.

LADIES' LUNCHEON

Many years ago, I was asked to speak at a luncheon of about 100 women at a local country club. My topic, of course, was skin care. I think I had about 15 minutes to impart my information to the female audience. The only other speaker was a local fashion stylist who spoke before me.

With only 15 minutes allotted for my presentation, I chose two topics that were popular at the time. (This was around 2010, I think.) As I recall, my topics were sun damage and wrinkles.

During the stylist's presentation, I was in the audience eating my lunch along with the 100 attendees. I noticed lunch was served as she spoke, and everyone continued to eat their meal throughout her presentation. The reason I was paying attention to these details is because I wanted to know what to expect when it was my turn at the podium.

When the stylist left the stage, I stepped up to begin my presentation. As I spoke, I looked over the audience expecting to find that nobody was looking at me. However, much to my surprise, what I saw was 100 women not eating the food on their plates. Their forks were down, and they were paying very close attention to my words.

At one point, I looked toward the back of the room beyond the lunch tables, and I realized that an additional group of people were standing in the rear listening to me. I figured out that the servers had stopped serving, bartenders had stopped bartending, and management had stopped managing, and they were all standing there listening to me. Of course, I'd love to believe it was because of my charm and eloquence, however, I know it was because the information I was giving was so relevant to the audience.

I kept my eye on the time, however when my 15 minutes were up, the questions kept coming. The ladies in the audience asked me so many questions that I ran out of time, and I was being signaled to stop talking. I knew it was time for me to go, but I wasn't sure how to do that gracefully without being rude to those who were so generously giving their attention to me. Fortunately, someone finally came up to the podium and announced that I would be available to answer more questions after lunch.

After lunch, I was bombarded! I stayed long after the event had ended to discuss skin care with the attendees. So many of them asked for my card or my contact information but unfortunately at that time in my career as a Solo Esthetician, I was not able to absorb all the women who wanted services from me.

And that, my fellow Estheticians, was a big "a-ha" moment in my life as an Esthetician. The big lesson for me that day was that there are so many women (and men) who really want to learn about good skin care and are willing to put in the effort to achieve their skin care goals, but unfortunately, they don't know how to do that. They do try though, by purchasing products they hear about from various online (and other) sources. But unless they have personal access to a qualified Esthetician, it is not likely they will receive accurate information related to their specific needs.

BeWELL EXPO

BeWell Expo was another of my big "a-ha" moments that changed everything in my career.

BeWell Expo was hosted by Les Nouvelles Esthetiques & Spa magazine, but it was not their usual trade show for Estheticians and spa professionals. As the name BeWell Expo implies, it was a wellness event for consumers (i.e., the general public) to introduce them to the world of spa and wellness. These events were held in California convention centers such as Los Angeles, Pasadena and Sacramento.

My role. I was the Director of the Skin Analysis Lounge at BeWell Expo. I brought in Estheticians to work with me and our goal was to bring clients into the Skin Analysis Lounge, sit down with them, and educate them about skin care. We utilized various high-tech skin analysis equipment which enabled us to impart some really good information to the attendees. What we did not know at the time was just how successful the Skin Analysis Lounge would be. We were swamped!

What I learned from this experience with hundreds of (mostly) women was that they are really interested in proper skin care! They want to know everything, and they are looking for information wherever they can find it.

Unfortunately, most women do not have easy access to an Esthetician. It is not like a department store where they can wander in and have a face-to-face conversation with someone. To have access to an Esthetician, they would have to make an appointment and have a facial. And sometimes they aren't ready for that.

Maybe they do not really understand what it is Estheticians do. In fact, I spent a lot of time at these BeWell Expo events explaining to women the role of an Esthetician.

Even if people are generally familiar with what Estheticians do, they may not personally know an Esthetician in their area. That means there are potential clients everywhere, and they are out there spending millions of dollars on products that are not nearly as good as our high-quality professional products. And these potential clients are spending all of this money on skin care products without the guidance of a licensed and trained Professional Esthetician.

So do not concern yourself with attracting new clients who are already actively getting facials somewhere. Instead, focus on ways you can make yourself available to those potential clients who do not yet know what you, a Professional Esthetician, can do for them.

CRAZY OLD AUNT IN THE ATTIC

We have covered how women show up. Now let's explore how you, the Esthetician, shows up: How you show up when you are out in the world, meeting potential clients, how you show up for your existing clients, and most importantly, how you show up for yourself.

This is a little exercise that I picked up when I was working at the Deepak Chopra Center. I liked this little exercise a lot, so I revised it to fit Estheticians and I am giving it to you below as Personal Development Tool #2.

That voice in your head – you know that voice that reprimands you and criticizes you? ("I can't. I'll never be able to do this. I'm not good at this. I'll never be successful. I'm not smart enough") Yeah, that's the one. It's like the annoying roommate that lives in your head rent-free.

All of these critiques running in a loop inside your head are more than likely things that somebody else told you about yourself. Maybe it's somebody you know....a family member, an employer, someone significant in your life. But no matter the source, we often pick this stuff up and carry it with us into every new chapter of our lives.

It is like dragging a heavy garbage bag filled with all the scars and bad memories of your life through every new doorway you enter. Do you realize you that do not have to do that anymore? This is a choice you are making (probably every day), and you can choose to leave that bag of junk outside the door before you walk through it. I assure you, it will still be there if you "need" it, if you have come to depend on it, or if it's a habit you are not yet ready to break. But if you can muster the courage to allow yourself to live even a single day without it, you will come to realize that you do not need it.

So remember this: Yes, we all have that voice. But that voice is NOT you! You are not your thoughts….you are simply the thinker of your thoughts, and there is a big difference. You have the power to change your thoughts, which will eliminate so many self-imposed obstacles in your life. Can you imagine how great that would feel?

Those mountains that you've been carrying...
you were only supposed to climb.

PERSONAL DEVELOPMENT TOOL #2
The Voice

Give the voice a name. Choose a name that will separate it from being YOU. I suggest making it a silly name, a condescending name, or a dismissive name. (I chose "Crazy Old Aunt in the Attic.") You can use cuss words, if you like, you can make it funny. Just be sure it is not a real person that you know. Do not make it personal.

Make a list. Write down the comments that pop into your head and keep the list handy so you can add comments that come to you as you continue through this book and beyond. Odds are very high that as you go through the lessons in this book, you will run up against obstacles. That is when the voice will say to you, "You can't do that,

DIANE BUCCOLA

that won't work." The only way to clear those pesky obstacles is to acknowledge that they are there.

The reason it is important to write these negative comments down is that by transferring them to paper, you are freeing your mind. Of course, those comments will be there if you need to refer back to them (just like that garbage bag you left at the door), but my hope is that seeing them written down might be just what you need to finally let them go for good.

In his/her voice. Be sure to write down these comments in someone else's voice, as if someone is telling it to you. In other words, begin the sentence with "you are…." rather than "I am…" because that voice is ***not you***.

18

DO YOU WANT TO MAKE A LIVING... OR CREATE A LIFE?

To anyone looking in from the outside, it may appear that it is the ability to make a living and a potential for profit that draws Estheticians into the field of esthetics. The observer might also think that an action-packed menu of services is the foundation for an Esthetician's financial success. But for those of us who are actually working in the treatment room, we know that in reality, it is <u>passion</u> that brings us here and it is <u>vision</u> that makes us successful.

I am going to make everything around me more beautiful.
That will be my life.
~Elise de Wolf

Now that you've identified that voice in your head, you have control over it. Your mind is open, and it is time to begin the process of curating your dream esthetics business. To do that, you must first be able to imagine it. To literally see it in your mind. So please grab something with which to make notes so you can record your thoughts and ideas as we go along.

When thinking about financial success, remember this: Money will not go anywhere it is not loved. By "loved" I don't mean "coveted." I mean you must feel valuable, you must not only welcome your financial success, but you have to be excited about it. In other words, every time you think or say to yourself (or others) "I don't have what it takes. I'm not enough. The money won't come," you are effectively keeping your financial success away. Please don't do that!

LIVING YOUR DREAM

Ultimate success comes from living your dream and doing the work because it is a passion -- not simply to earn enough money to survive.

Passion for your work means that you would do it even if you were paid no money, because you just can't help yourself. Quite simply, you love it. So let's start there.

Passion

I would like you to think back to why you were initially drawn to a career in esthetics…and as always, there is no right or wrong answer. I have asked this question of many Estheticians over the years, and the answer is almost always the same. It is typically something along the lines of, "I like to help people feel good." Sound familiar? If that is your answer also, well then, therein lies your *passion*.

> *If you have a "passion," good for you! Many people don't.*
> *If you don't have a passion, just follow your curiosity…*
> *and watch for the breadcrumbs leading you forward.*

And now, Vision

It is imperative that you do not allow your vision to be affected by other Estheticians or spas. Just because an Esthetician or spa appears to be very busy, very well-known, or ever-expanding, does not by any means indicate that they are financially successful. And trust me, most business owners are not going to 'fess up to failures, so unless you have a look at their accounting records, you cannot possibly determine the extent of another's financial success.

The word "success" means many things to many people. Some simply want to have their name on the door and be a celebrity in their own town (or in their own mind). Others may view it as a part-time gig that fits in with their lifestyle. But this is about you, and only you can determine your definition of success.

PERSONAL DEVELOPMENT TOOL #3
What is your definition of "Success"?

Consider (and write down) the answer to this question: What does "success" mean to ME?

There are no correct answers here because this is your definition, this is your dream, this is your career. Just write down whatever pops into your head…and please dream big. Really big.

- Could it be having your name on the door? If that is your definition, then imagine your name illuminated, big and bright, imagine it in the newspaper (on the front page, of course!).
- Is it financial reward? If so, imagine so much money that an armored truck has to pull up at the front of your business and drop it off.
- Is it a full client book? In your mind, make it bigger than a book. Make it a library with volumes of client appointments over multiple years.

I know, this sounds so silly. But what we are trying to do here is shake awake your dreams, see your vision and feel your passion. And if you come up with visuals like armored trucks or neon signs, your name in lights, that's great. If it is grandiose enough that it causes you to laugh, all the better because that is what good energy feels like. And good energy can make monumental things happen.

Miracles start to happen when you give as much energy to your dreams
as you do to your fears.
~Richard Wilkins

The real reason we do not move creatively ahead is always and only fear. "I don't have the skills, I don't have the right, my idea has already been done…better. I'll be criticized or ignored. What's the point?" The solution for putting these fears behind you is simply that you must accept the fact that so much of what we do, we have learned from others. And conversely, others have (or will) learn much of what they do from you. So yes, it has already been done…but it has not yet been done by you. We are all just borrowing from each other, and you are allowed to add to the pile.

Too many of us are afraid of our creativity because creativity will always provoke fear. But fear is actually a necessary companion. Fear should be viewed with a tremendous amount of respect and appreciation. Fear is the reason we are alive today. Every single one of us can point to a moment in our lives that we survived something because we were afraid. Fear warned us to "get out of that ocean, the waves are too big" or "this car is going too fast" or "this street is not safe to walk down" Our fear is constantly protecting us. That is its job.

So, allow fear to have a seat in the car as you build your dream esthetics business, but put it in the back seat. It will not drive, and it will not make any decisions. You cannot let fear have any control over your creative choices or else it will shut them down, one idea after another. "Nope, don't do that. Nope, too risky." And your life will be so much smaller than you want your life to be.

I commit to enjoying my esthetics career
and my financial well-being to my full potential.
(~you)

KNOW THYSELF

What do you love <u>most</u> about esthetics?

If you are a working Esthetician, you have a lot to pull from as a result of experiences you have had in the treatment room from which to answer this question. And if you are an esthetics student, or recently licensed Esthetician, think about what you liked best about your esthetics program.

It could be that you love performing specific services. Or it could be that, like me, what you like best is interacting with clients. Some of you are more like chemists than I ever was. You understand ingredients and carry an ingredient dictionary in your brain. Many of my Esthetician friends can have detailed scientific conversations about ingredients that just blows my mind. I, on the other hand, often had to refer to books to figure things out. Or maybe you just generally like making people feel good. That is a marvelous thing to love about the esthetics business.

What do you love <u>least</u> about esthetics?

Of course, we must also consider the things we do not necessarily love about esthetics. It could be that you don't like selling products or marketing yourself in order to get new clients. Maybe you dislike taking inventory, managing employees, dealing with taxes.

For me, it was leg waxing. I hated leg waxing. I hate to use the word "hate" but I really hated leg waxing. I used soft wax in the pot, and it was so sticky and so messy. I almost always ended up with wax in my hair, on my lab coat, on the floor. The truth is, because I did not like leg waxing, I wasn't great at it. So when I got successful enough, I just stopped doing it. And I was so relieved!

There are many ways to eliminate services that you do not like to do. For example, you can refer out to someone else, or you can bring in another Esthetician who loves leg waxing (or whatever service you despise). Have her or him come in once a week to do your clients' leg waxing. Remember, you will be best, most successful, and happiest doing the things you love.

PERSONAL DEVELOPMENT TOOL #4
Your Vision

The best place to start in preparation for creating your dream esthetics business is to assess where you are right now. Here is a list of questions to get you started.

The first question is "What does my successful esthetics business look like in mind?" Visualize it in great detail and write it down. For example, how many employees, how many treatment rooms, what your monthly sales will be, what color are the walls, what will your specialty be?

Be sure to spend extra time on numbers 7 and 8 because they are super important.

1. What does my successful esthetics business look like in my mind? (Visualize it.)
2. On a 1-10 scale (with #1 being "Not even in the ballpark, honey!"), how close am I to my vision?
3. Are my current efforts taking me in the direction I want to go?
4. What am I currently doing that *is* working toward my vision?
5. What am I currently doing that is *not* working toward my vision?
6. What obstacles to my success can I identify right now?
7. Who around me is influencing me at this time?
8. Is this a positive or negative influence?

THE ROAD TO IMPROVEMENT

The road to improvement is much simpler than you probably think it is. For many of us, our mind automatically goes to all the hard work that must be done, the actions that must be taken, and the volume of effort we must put in. But oftentimes, that type of thought is less about reality and more about how our mind is processing information... about our dreams, our plans, our expectations and most importantly, our confidence.

She who argues her limitations gets to keep them: You can offer suggestions to someone, but if they push back with all the reasons that it will not work, you just have to let it go. If they believe it will not work, then it will not work for them. The same goes for you: If your instinct is to argue all the reasons why you cannot have a successful esthetics career, then that is how it will be for you. This is a choice that only you can make. Nobody can make it for you.

Do not constantly take score: Don't compare yourself. In fact, don't even share your plans with anyone unless and until it becomes absolutely necessary. Of course, there will come a point where you will want input, advice and expertise from others. However, when you are just beginning to dream a bit, maybe formulating plans, often that is not the best time to ask for input because your advisor might shoot you down based upon his or her own perceived limitations.

Look through the windshield, not the rear-view mirror: This is symbolism meaning the reason the windshield is larger than the rear-view mirror is that you are meant to look forward, not backward.

Do not point to old scars: Do not reignite past mistakes or injuries. Do not give those missteps power over your today. Of course, take with you any lessons you learned from those experiences, but don't also bring along the scars.

It is not your job to have an opinion about what others believe: Those opinions are not you, and sometimes people don't want you to outshine them. So again, don't ask for opinions until you really need someone's expert advice. Trust yourself.

Guide your life, do not let it guide you: You are the driver of this vehicle, so assume control. You know **you** better than anyone else does. Learn to listen to your own instincts.

Live, laugh, learn: Enjoy the process. There is much to learn, and there are many directions you will turn as you follow the path to your dream esthetics career. Enjoy it. You deserve the fun.

Think differently: Basically, if you keep thinking the same thoughts, especially if they are reinforced by others, then everything is going to remain the same. That is the reason for these lists you been making. This is why I have asked you to write all of this down. It clears your mind and blocks out the voices of others. Only then will you have full access to ideas that you come up with on your own.

Don't look back. You're not going that way.

Pearls of Wisdom

- If you changed only 1% per week, by year's end you would be 52% (more than halfway!) to your goal.
- It's not how much money you make that counts, it's how much money you get to keep!
- A busy spa does not necessarily mean a financially successful spa.
- Let the views of others educate and inform you, but don't model yourself after other spas and other Estheticians.
- Don't be afraid to be different....and better.

3 THE PROFESSIONAL ESTHETICIAN

ESTHETICIAN'S "JOBS"

When we first enter the esthetics business, we may think our primary job will be providing facial services, but after a while we realize that it's a lot more than that. Every successful Esthetician knows that wearing many "hats" is part of the job.

- **Analyst** – This of course is our most important job and it's what separates us from all the others. We use our education, training and licensure to analyze our client's current skin condition and customize a treatment plan according to his or her specific skin care needs.
- **Scientist** – These skills are called upon regularly to assist us when assessing ingredients and recognizing possible contraindications.
- **Psychic** – If you have clients who buy products from you, then you have had the experience wherein clients will call, email or text when they want to replenish their home care supply. However, instead of giving you the proper name of the product, they will say something like "it's that clear liquid that comes in a brown bottle and has a dropper, and the writing is gold." That's when you must tap into your psychic skills to figure out which product they are referring to. Of course, if you are keeping detailed records on each of your

clients, you will be able to figure it out quickly, but mind reading is a skill that Estheticians do utilize occasionally.

- **Techie** – How about when a piece of equipment ships with less than optimum instructions? Or when equipment stops working in the middle of a service? And then there are websites that we are required to manage and keep updated. A Techie hat is definitely required for these tasks.

- **Administrator** – Record keeping, note taking, appointment scheduling, ordering, shipping, processing payment. We do it all.

- **Consultant** – Have you ever been in a social gathering with women and not talked about skin care services, products, wrinkles, anti-aging, etc.? If you're anything like me, the answer is a NO.

- **Wizard** – Well, that's just because we make magic happen. The Esthetician Magician!

- **Friend** – Over the long duration of my esthetics career, I have been part of landmark moments in my clients' lives. Some of those landmarks include weddings, divorces, new babies, death in the family, important decisions and therapy sessions. It has been an honor and a privilege.

- **Parent** – Children of clients have come to me for various facial services and hair removal services over the years. In many cases, by virtue of my relationship with these young people, I ended up knowing more about their personal lives than their parents did! I have watched them grow up, date, get married, and have babies and I have been invited to the weddings and celebratory showers. What a joy!

- **Advisor** – For me, this is evidenced by my career as an author, speaker and mentor. It is the chapter of my esthetics career that I love most.

- **Cheerleader** – It is always a good feeling to have a positive impact on clients and know that I had a part in helping them feel fabulous.

ENERGY & BALANCE

For the last couple of decades, energy work has been gaining in popularity in the spa industry. In this section, I am referring to the art of balancing your personal energy.

Methods of Balancing Energy

Taking steps to balance your energy will keep you healthy and stress-free. Although your goal is to protect yourself from your clients' unbalanced energy, the client will also enjoy the benefit of your balanced energy. Here is a short list of energy-balancing methods:

- Meditation
- Grounding/Earthing
- Visualization
- Affirmations
- Reiki
- Feng Shui
- Aromatherapy
- Subliminal audio
- Negative ions/salt lamps

I expect many of you are already familiar with many items on this list and quite possibly are already using some of these in your esthetics practice. For example, I know a lot of us use aromatherapy, and some of us (like me) are Reiki certified. But perhaps there are a few others that you may not be as familiar with.

Grounding. As a newly-licensed Esthetician, I learned the importance of "grounding." However, back then, I understood that to mean the process of standing at the head of my facial bed and visualizing roots coming from my feet and traveling down into the earth, thereby connecting my energy and "grounding" me. The reason energy and balance are significant is because the situation with our clients in the treatment room is so close and intimate. Because of this, we risk the transference of energy, either theirs to us or ours to them.

When you are exposed to a client with a negative attitude or perhaps someone in your life happens to be in a bad mood, that energy can directly impact your entire day -- in and out of your treatment room -- and it can be passed along to other clients. And worst of all, you can take that energy home with you and it can impact your personal life. This is why Estheticians must learn methods to maintain balance and practice their preferred method(s) on a daily basis.

> **Think of energy balancing it this way:** You wouldn't dream of leaving your home without brushing your teeth because you know it is a matter of dental hygiene. Similarly, balancing your energy before you leave your house (or before your first client arrives) is energetic hygiene. Without it, you are at the mercy of the energy you will undoubted encounter throughout your day… like being in a rowboat with no oars, and therefore no control as to the direction you will go.

As a new Esthetician, I also learned about the benefits of negative ions which are molecules that have been charged with electricity. Oddly enough, negative ions create positive vibes which seems counter-intuitive, but that is how it works. If you have been to the ocean, then you have experienced the wonderful energy of negative ions provided by sea air. That's why everyone feels so good near the ocean. So when you are at the beach, be sure to remove your shoes and walk in the sand and/or the ocean. Or take a walk in the grass. Besides feeling really good on your feet, it's actually really good for you.

Subliminal audio. Affirmations and meditation are self-explanatory and are typically used outside of the treatment room; however, there are ways to incorporate these techniques into your esthetics practice if they appeal to you. As an example, subliminal music is something in which the client is hearing spa music but there are subliminal affirmations going on beneath the surface of the sound.

I used to offer specific facials wherein the client would be wearing earbuds to listen to subliminal music rather than traditional spa music. With earbuds in, I could not do everything I would normally do in a regular facial, but this was a specific treatment for which they had to sign a consent form to acknowledge that they understood the components of this service.[1] Some of the more popular subliminal options were related to de-stressing.

Salt lamps. It is a common belief that salt lamps also produce negative ions so I always had a salt lamp in my treatment room and one in my office. As a new Esthetician, I learned that salt lamps can help counteract the positive ions (bad energy) coming from the electrical equipment in our treatment room. Whether or not that's true, salt lamps give off a lovely amber light, and that's good enough for me.

I am grounded, centered and present.
(~you)

---

[1] *Include with the Consent Form a printed version of the words being spoken within subliminal music.*

LICENSED ESTHETICIAN v. PROFESSIONAL ESTHETICIAN

The "Professional Esthetician" is not an actual license, of course. It is a term that I am using to distinguish between an Esthetician who obtains his or her license and does not evolve beyond that point, and an Esthetician who goes on to reach elevated levels in his or her esthetics career.

LEVEL 1: The Licensed Esthetician

Obviously, we all start out as a Licensed Esthetician, and sticking with that is a perfectly fine choice, as long as you are following the laws that govern your license and you do not hurt anyone. However, in my two+ decades in the esthetics business, I have come to realize that there is another level of licensed Esthetician which includes a much higher level of responsibility.

The Licensed Esthetician's minimum responsibilities and privileges are:

- Met the state's training hours requirement
- Passed the state's licensing exam
- Permitted to provide services within scope of state license
- Allowed to purchase professional skin care products at wholesale prices
- Allowed to sell professional skin care products
- Permitted to attend professional esthetics & spa trade shows
- May legally refer to themselves according to what is stated on their license

To sum up: A Licensed Esthetician has met the state's minimum training hours requirement and they have successfully passed the state's licensing exam. So now they are permitted to provide services within the scope of their state license, and they are permitted to purchase skin care products at wholesale prices and sell them as retail products to their clients. A Licensed Esthetician is allowed to attend professional esthetics and spa trade shows and they are legally allowed to refer to themselves as whatever title is written on their state license. For example, for me, it would be "Esthetician" while in other states, it might be spelled "Aesthetician."

LEVEL 2: The Professional Esthetician

We have already gone over the responsibilities and privileges granted to a Licensed Esthetician and now we are going to go over what makes a Professional Esthetician a more elevated role in the field of esthetics. The Professional Estheticians understands that we are not in the "facial" business. We are in the "skin care" business. This is a very big and very important distinction.

As you can see in the list below, a Professional Esthetician has more responsibilities. While these responsibilities are not forced upon them by their license, ultimately these Estheticians carry a much heavier burden. They are leading the way and raising the standards for all of us in the field of esthetics.

(I want to reiterate that "Professional Esthetician" is not an official license. It is simply a name that I am using here to represent an elevated version of a Licensed Esthetician. Of course, there are Estheticians who fall in between these 2 categories.)

- Met the state's minimum training hours requirement
- Passed the state's licensing exam
- Permitted to provide services within scope of state license
- Allowed to purchase professional skin care products at wholesale prices
- Allowed to sell professional skin care products
- Permitted to attend professional esthetics & spa trade shows
- May legally refer to themselves according to what is stated on their license
- Keeps herself/himself and her/his clients educated

- Does not use or sell Multi-Level Marketing (MLM) skin care products
- Is well-trained in skin analysis and skin conditions
- Gets to know her/his client's skin
- Understands ingredients, fillers, etc.
- Always does a proper intake and keeps good records
- Always uses consent forms
- Knows the laws of her/his state and stays within the course and scope of her/his license
- Communicates with clients beyond text and email
- Does not elevate the title of her/his licensure
- Does not sell professional products online to the general public

Keeps herself and her clients educated. Clients do not have the time, interest, or access to the depth of skin care information that Estheticians do. Let's be honest, if a potential client is not already seeing an Esthetician regularly, they are likely getting their information from television, magazines or department store salespeople….or from random advisors online. If Estheticians keep themselves well educated by taking continuing education classes and attending professional trade shows, they can pass along so much essential information to their clients. In other words, our clients can rest assured that we are out there keeping ourselves updated and educated so they don't have to!

Doesn't use or sell MLM products. Why would someone go through the effort and cost to earn an Esthetician license and then sell Multi-Level Marketing skin care products? Professional Estheticians are educated about ingredients, sourcing, fillers, skin conditions, hormonal fluctuations, and all of those other variables. MLM products are just a bad choice for an Professional Esthetician. Leave MLM products to the MLM salespeople. Let's just stay in our own lane and be great at what we do.

Is well-trained in skin analysis and skin conditions. This is so important. Let's be honest, anyone can give a facial. We all had to do it in order to get through Esthetician school. But to determine which is the best facial for our client based upon factors such as which ingredients are best for his or her skin condition on that particular day takes continuing education and training. Even when we think we know everything, a client's skin condition will change due to so many variables. To best help our clients with their constantly changing skin, we must keep up. The Professional Esthetician knows this.

Gets to know her client's skin. This is another thing that separates a Professional Esthetician (by far) from salespeople: There is no one-size-fits-all in skin care. The best facial for a client one month may not be the right choice the next month. Professional Estheticians can use their vast knowledge to vary services and home care regimens according to the client's ever-changing needs.

Understands ingredients, fillers, etc. This is what will always keep us way ahead of our competition. And by "competition" I mean wannabe Estheticians (aka salespeople). It is our level of ongoing education, training, experience and knowledge of the nuances of the skin, as well as skin care products' impact on the skin at any given time that differentiates us from the others. A Professional Esthetician's level of knowledge is something that salespeople cannot possibly reach.

Always does a proper intake and keeps good records. I apologize in advance for how many times you are going to hear me say this…but it really is so important. There are no shortcuts here. Record-keeping is not primarily about results. It is about safety. Every time an Esthetician harms someone because they did not ask all the right questions of a client before a service, the reputations of Estheticians everywhere are forever tarnished.

Uses consent forms. Once again, SO important. And so easy. This is about safety. And you could also say it's about covering your behind!

Knows the laws of her state and stays within the course and scope of her license Yikes, this is a big one! It is shocking how little some Estheticians know about what they can and cannot legally do under the laws of their license. This is yet another safety issue. A Professional Esthetician knows that there is no blaming the client if an Esthetician hurts someone.

Communicates with clients beyond text and email. I know online scheduling is wonderful. Those of us who started in this business before online scheduling probably appreciate it more than those who grew up with it. However, there is a downside, and it's a big one. Online scheduling, online appointment reminders, online follow-ups, etc., have eliminated the opportunity to personally connect with our clients outside of their presence in our treatment room. The odds of attracting potential clients through online communication has diminished enormously. That may not matter to 99% of other businesses, but a Professional Esthetician knows that ours is a very personal business which is based on -- and made successful by -- our personal relationships with clients (and potential clients).

Does not self-title. A Licensed Esthetician is not legally allowed to self-title with things like "Clinical Esthetician" or "Medical Esthetician." Or "Master Esthetician" if that is not what is written on their official state license. A Professional Esthetician knows that identifying herself or himself by anything other than what is written on her or his state license may be breaking the law. You could also call this "false advertising."

Does not sell products online to the public. IMO, this is the biggest threat to the field of esthetics. It is not about Amazon's online sales. It's about the Estheticians who use their licenses to purchase wholesale from our professional skin care product vendors, and then sell those products to anyone without so much as a consultation. This tarnishes and diminishes the reputation of all Estheticians, which is something a Professional Esthetician would never do.

EVER-EVOLVING ESTHETICS

In this section, I will give you a quick look back at what esthetics was like when I started as compared to how esthetics looks today. There is a big difference between those two eras and understanding the foundation that today's esthetics was built upon will ultimately make you a better Esthetician today.

I will also share some of the highlights of my esthetics career that I think may help you along your path to financial success.

ESTHETICS THEN

Estheticians who are coming out of esthetics school today may not be familiar with some of the principal elements on which esthetics was built, and it is those elements that helped turn esthetics into the booming business it is today. We will revisit some of those elements, beginning with Spa Products.

Products. When I started my spa in 2000, there weren't a lot of professional skin care product line options. Certainly, no clinical products were available to Estheticians, so our options were products that smelled really good and were packaged beautifully, but they didn't really do a heck of a lot. These products were better than bath soap, of course, but they were not necessarily giving huge results for our clients. Definitely nothing like the results that we see today.

Service Menu. Our menus were simple. We all had an "anti-aging facial" on our service menu, which is an oxymoron because there really is no "anti" in aging. We are going to age…there's no "anti" about it. It's how we do it that matters, and that is an Esthetician's specialty.

I had a "Deep Cleanse Facial" on my menu back then, and I used that mainly for men or clients with oily or acneic skin. I had a "Teen

37

Facial" and a "European Facial." I also offered microdermabrasion, which is not something I was taught in my Esthetician licensing program.

I had a glycolic peel on the menu because glycolic was the only AHA I learned about in esthetics school.

In those days, Esthetician programs were bare because there just wasn't much training available. So while we were somewhat competent when we graduated, we were not very well-trained. For example, the only esthetic equipment we learned about in my Esthetician program was high frequency. There was also a galvanic machine at my school, but it didn't work. So the teacher just pointed it out to us and told us what it was. It was just a very basic education, to say the least.

In 2000, there was really no internet to speak of. Dial-up was just coming on the scene and it was slow and frustrating. And the only Amazon at the time was a river in South America.

Back then, we steamed everyone. In other words, every facial service came with a steaming whether the client needed it or not. With the help of post-graduate education, I eventually figured out that not every facial needed steam.

The good news about esthetics back then is that professional skin care products were accessible only through Estheticians. Unfortunately, that is not the case these days. Throughout this book, I will take a look at that dilemma from various angles.

When I was in Esthetician school, we were taught many facial massage techniques because a "nice touch" was a central element of a facial. I'm not saying facial massage is not important now. What I am saying is that we have so many more clinical facial options in today's esthetics, many of which do not include facial massage.

We need to take words like "indulge" and "pamper"
out of the Spa Industry.
It is self-care and it is necessary.

"DAY SPA" MENTALITY

First of all, let me clarify: I do not mean we have to take "indulge" and "pamper" completely out of the skin care industry. What I mean is that when I started, we were all "day spas," and the goal of a day spa is to be all things to all people. In other words, we were attempting to bring to our neighborhoods the resort spa experience that most of us would have only while on vacation.

The words "spa" and "day spa" made perfect sense 15-20 years ago, but today the words "spa" and "day spa" are overused and abused and very often do not fit the actual "day spa" model. The "day spa" experience is meant to be spa services you can have in one day. Typically, a day spa offered massage services, body treatments, esthetics services, sometimes nail and hair services. It's a beautiful thought and it's a lovely experience. However, today esthetics has become more clinical, and therefore we have so many more options regarding equipment, protocols and products.

Anybody who is considering opening an esthetics business today or is struggling with their current business may need to rethink whether they really need to be all things to all people. Today you are free to call your esthetics business something other than a "spa" or "day spa" which gives you the ability to stand out from all the other day spas.

ESTHETICS NOW

Moving now to today's esthetics where everything has become much more clinical. We have amazing high-tech equipment and stronger active ingredients in our products. The downside of that development however is that we are now able to hurt people more easily and more often than we could previously.

Esthetics is no longer limited to "fluff and puff" services provided by cosmetologists; in fact, it is no longer associated with hair and cosmetology services at all. But with that, and all the paths we can now take in the field of esthetics, more often rules are broken, laws are not followed, and clients are more likely to be harmed. This makes it essential that Estheticians know the laws of their state at all times and are well-versed about what is included within the course and scope of their license.

Home Use. One of the more frustrating aspects of this continued rapid growth is that many of the "professional" equipment and tools we use in the treatment room are now readily available for home use. It seems as though almost immediately after a new professional tool or equipment comes out, a home use version comes out as well.

Over the years, as soon as a piece of professional equipment I was using in the treatment room became available for home use, I immediately stopped using it. The first one that happened with for me was the Clarisonic rotary brush. I didn't use that very often because I knew that manual exfoliation is not necessarily the best choice for all clients. So I reserved that equipment for teens and younger skin, as well as services for men and backs, and the moment that tool became available for home use, I dropped it and moved on to something else.

We want clients to come to us for services that they can't do at home, so watch out for tools and equipment that becomes available for home use. Those Estheticians who keep an eye on up-and-coming tools and techniques will always be one step ahead of the competition. This is another great reason to attend our professional esthetics trade shows where you can see what procedures, equipment and products are coming next. Then you can get trained and bring new things into your esthetics business. Sell your no-longer-needed equipment and keep moving forward into the future of esthetics.

When you see how far esthetics has come from then to now, it makes sense that wise Estheticians will try to figure out which way esthetics is going and where it might be in 5 or 10 years. Research what other states and other countries are doing because it will get to your city at some point.

> *Change is good for us and good for our clients.*
> *There is nothing worse than being boring....and bored.*

OBSTACLES

There will always be obstacles around us at any given time in work and in life, so it is crucial that we be prepared. However, some of those obstacles you have been warned about, or read about, are not real or will not apply to you. On the other hand, there are some important obstacles that we can (and should) remove from our path. So, what are the obstacles that may get in the way of an Esthetician's success?

I will give you my short list of perceived obstacles, and I suggest that you write down some of your own if you think of any that aren't on my list. You might be surprised at what you find when you look back at your list after reading this book. Having written them down all in one place, you might discover that those obstacles do not have as much power as you originally attributed to them.

Often in the winds of change, a new direction is found.

COMPETITION

It used to be that having good products and an interesting menu was enough to lure clients to your esthetics business, and to keep them coming back. You didn't even have to be particularly skilled in the treatment room. However, as day spas gained in popularity, clients became more discriminating. As a result, today's Estheticians are literally competing with every business that sells absolutely anything.

Doctors. When I entered the spa business, there were no medi-spas. But now, every kind of doctor has a spa, such as gynecologists, internists, dentists, you name it! But often, a doctor's medi-spa is geared towards luring a client in for a facial and then moving him or her up to more aggressive treatments or surgical procedures.

When people I meet ask me about skin care, I reply with my best advice which is: "Start with an Esthetician who is trained well and can consult with you, analyze your skin, explain skin care to you, and get you on a good facial schedule with professional products being used at home. Try that for a few months, and then if you feel you need to go up to a more aggressive procedure or surgery, by all means, consult a board-certified medical doctor."

Most of the time, consumers do not realize what an Esthetician can do for them and why an Esthetician is such a great place to start. An important part of our job is to educate clients, potential clients and the public.

Multi-Level-Marketing. If you are an Esthetician who is on social media, have email or a phone, then you have likely crossed paths with a Multi-Level-Marketing skin care product salesperson (also known by other titles such as "brand ambassador.") These are the home party people who are on the lookout for Estheticians who might be willing to cross to the other side and become involved with an MLM. This is a bonus for the MLM'er because partnering with a licensed Esthetician may give them credibility that they wouldn't otherwise enjoy.

I know it is so frustrating for Estheticians to constantly be contacted by these people offering us an "opportunity." Do they not realize that every one of them uses the exact same company-scripted sales pitch? And do they not know that Estheticians have been down this road sooooo many times before, certainly every time a new MLM comes on the scene.

With the rare exception of a wayward Esthetician who gets involved in these things, MLM people are not competition for us. They are not trained as we are, they don't have the educational opportunities that we do, nor are they licensed Estheticians. So let them do their thing, but if you are a Professional Esthetician (or want to be), stay away from MLM skin care companies and products.

As an Esthetician, you will come to understand that there is room for all of us in the world of skin care, and there really is no need for a great Esthetician to worry about this type of competition. If we stay in our lane and they stay in their lane, we can peacefully co-exist. We've been doing it successfully for years.

Department Stores. Department store salespeople are easily accessible to consumers, whereas consumers do not have the same easy access to Estheticians. Consumers can walk into a department store and find plenty of salespeople ready to discuss skin care with them and talk them into buying whatever brand they might be selling that day.

This is a legit disadvantage to Estheticians in that we are not standing in public places waiting for people to wander by and talk to us. For this reason, we must put ourselves in environments where we will have access to people who are interested in skin care.

Grocery Store/Drug Store. These shoppers need us the most because as Estheticians, we know what is in the products on those shelves. Of course, the packaging says all the right things, but Estheticians know about ingredients, sourcing, fillers, etc., which means we know better. Estheticians also know that products sold randomly over-the-counter to the public must be neutral and relatively inactive so that people do not harm themselves and sue somebody.

The Economy. You might want to blame the economy for sluggish sales or sluggish bookings but actually the economy works in the favor of Estheticians. This is because those clients who were previously able to afford pricey medical procedures are now looking for more affordable options, and that leads them directly to Estheticians.

As the economy fluctuates, perhaps we will need to adjust our client base, adjust our menus, maybe get more clinical training in some areas, and consider adding advanced treatments and abbreviated facials to our menu. But the fluctuating economy traditionally works in our favor as opposed to against us.

Sometimes the grass is greener on the other side...
because it's fake.

Magic products. Consumers see ads for one-size-fits-all products with scientific-sounding ingredients which often are marketed by celebrities. This kind of marketing targets women in an effort to have them believe outrageous claims, for example that a single serum would be good for all skin types and conditions. As Estheticians, we know that is not how it works.

In addition to being the spokesperson for skin care lines, many celebrities have their own skin care lines now. And the celebrity whose name is on the skin care line (who has likely been airbrushed and tweaked to perfection by a glam squad) wants women to believe that a monthly delivery of these magic products is going to change their life. Because "celebrities are just like us," right?

Unfortunately, too many consumers do not understand that without an in-person skin analysis by a licensed and trained skin care professional, in a treatment room, utilizing his or her esthetic training, tools and equipment, it is impossible to determine which skin care products and home care protocols are best for optimum skin health which will result in achieving the client's preferred results.

As Estheticians, our ammunition is our training and the endless opportunities for continuing education. Anyone who has ever had an actual facial by a really well-trained and licensed Esthetician knows that our intake process is very different from a salesperson looking at a person's skin in a department store or an MLM home party. Department store, grocery store, MLM salespeople cannot do anything even close to what an Esthetician can do for their clients.

Big box advertising v. Esthetician budget. Estheticians do not advertise on TV or in magazines. We do not put signs on busses, benches and billboards. Therefore, consumers may not really understand what it is we do. This is the reason that consumers often go from washing their face with bar soap directly to surgical remedies, without a pitstop at a local Esthetician.

Self-Limitations. And then there are the self-imposed limitations, the ones we place on ourselves. For example, we might have convinced ourselves that we are losing clients because we do not have a huge budget with which to advertise. But you know what? The clients who would be swayed by the big box skin care companies are not the type of clients we want anyway. Those clients have low standards, and the clients we want have high standards; they are high quality and loyal.

Fear of marketing and fear of selling. We are going to go into this in great detail later in this book but for now, I just would like to say that I know this to be true: In my over two decades in the esthetics business, I have never met one Esthetician who got into this business to "sell." Yet fear of sales is an obstacle and a burden for many Estheticians.

You will learn later in this book that selling home care products is not about "sales" at all. It is about providing your clients with home care protocols and products that will extend the life of the facial. There is no need to talk anybody into buying anything. Home care sales will happen organically, and I am going to teach you exactly how that works.

Online sales. It appears to be an insurmountable obstacle if you are comparing esthetics today to esthetics 20 years ago. But online sales are here to stay so there is no need to waste time and energy fretting and complaining about it. What you can do is learn how to work with it instead of pushing against it.

Estheticians know that it is not simply products that bring about optimum skin health. It is a result of a combination of things beginning with a proper initial evaluation which is the only way to determine the client's current skin condition, followed by a comprehensive consultation in which vital info is gathered from the client. Very specific esthetic services can then be determined based upon the evaluation and the consultation. And all of this is supported by proper home care.

THINGS TO CONSIDER: "MISTAKES"

Things to Consider. I am not a fan of the word "mistake" because things that may go wrong occasionally are actually lessons that propel us in a different direction. We learn, we adjust, or perhaps we completely change something, which usually turns out to be for the best, and which would not have happened if not for the "mistake."

That said, some of these obstacles can be avoided just by being aware of them. So rather than "mistakes," I'm going to use the phrase "things to consider." These are things you may have no idea are happening but once you are aware, you can decide if an adjustment might be called for.

Below are topics I have seen first-hand…and quite frankly, I've done some of these myself, so I know they can be avoided once you become aware of them. The insight you gain can be used as a tool to help you create a client list that is packed – not just with clients, but with raving fans.

Just remember that clients do not typically leave because the service was not good. They leave because either they did not get what they were expecting, or they did not feel cared for.

There's nothing wrong with making mistakes.
What's wrong is letting the mistake remain,
without an effort to make it right.

Attitude

You might think that having a good vibe in your treatment room involves dim lighting with flickering candles and soothing music. That is all very nice, of course, but those elements pale in comparison to the impact the Esthetician's personal energy can have on a client.

When a client comes to us, there is a lot going on besides skin care. There is an energy exchange between you and your client. There is a matter of trust between you and your client; in other words, a lot rides on how the client feels when he or she is with you.

Some of the most telling experiences I have had as a consultant are when I interact with a spa's clientele in some capacity. When the clients understand that I am not an official employee of the spa, nor am I connected to management of the spa, they often feel compelled to tell me their true feelings about experiences they have had with a service, with a staff member, or with a licensed technician. I often get quite an earful.

Because I am a licensed Esthetician and a former spa owner, I can understand what is at the heart of the problem. More often than not, the issue is not with the specifics of the facial service. Nor is it about the price, the products, or the comfort of the facial bed. Rather, it is almost always related to an unpleasant attitude or negative vibe coming from the Esthetician.

This happens a lot in spas but unfortunately in most cases, neither the spa owner nor the Esthetician will ever learn the source of the client's discomfort because the client will just quietly fade away, leaving the Esthetician or spa to incorrectly place blame on something external like the economy or local competition. Because rarely does anyone follow up with clients who have gone M.I.A., the important lessons that could come from this situation are gone forever...as is the client.

Sometimes you have to tell the negative committee that meets inside your head to shut up.

BlahBlahBlah

This is a tricky one, but it is something we must consider because it is very common. Oftentimes when a client mysteriously disappears, it could very well be because there was too much talking going on during the facial. The issue typically is that the client would prefer to have quiet during the facial, but in our effort to be friendly or helpful, we miss the client's cues. In some cases, we have become friends with our clients, so we are excited to see them and we have a lot to chat about.

This is not entirely the fault of the Esthetician because our clients are willing participants. Not only will they happily talk back to us, but oftentimes they are the ones who initiate the conversation. But truth be told, once the service has begun what they really want is peace and quiet.

I will share with you the way I navigated this obstacle. But first let me stop and say that this does not apply to new clients because at a first-time appointment, we have a lot of essential information that we must extract and impart. And for that reason, it's a good idea to tell new clients up front: "Because this is your first appointment with me, I'm going to give you a lot of information…but in subsequent facials, that won't be necessary." Which translates to: "There will be a lot of conversation this time but after that, the amount of conversation is up to you (the client)."

After I have said whatever it is I need to say to the new client and I have asked whatever questions I need to ask, then I will say: I have given you the information you need to know at this point…now, I'm just going to be quiet and let you relax and enjoy your facial. However, if you have any questions for me, please feel free to ask and I will be happy to answer."

And then just see how it goes. If they continue to talk, then you know quiet is not a priority for this client. But if they go silent and remain silent, then you'll know that they prefer quiet. Be sure to make a note somewhere in their file so that you can always provide the personalized experience that each client prefers.

Being "good enough" is no longer good enough.

NEUTRALIZING OF ESTHETICIANS

neu-tra-lize
verb
"render (something) ineffective by applying an opposite force or effect."

ELIMINATING ESTHETICIANS
FROM THE SKIN CARE EQUATION

It would be wonderful if we could blame somebody else for the neutralizing of Estheticians, but you know who is the biggest culprit? Estheticians! Think about that for a moment.

We want clients and the general public to believe that we are trained esthetics professionals, that we are educated in esthetics and knowledgeable about skin conditions, that we use the highest-quality professional skin care products, and that we are trained to know which products and which treatments will provide optimal results for clients based upon all the variables which we are educated about.

We want clients to believe that they can trust us and rely on our guidance. In essence, we want them to believe, as we do, that Estheticians are a very necessary component of their skin care journey.

However, when a licensed Esthetician is giving facials without first requiring a detailed consultation, skin analysis and intake process -- in other words, no detailed gathering of important information -- or when an Esthetician is selling professional skin care products on Amazon or on their own open-to-the-public e-store, or when an Esthetician is uploading all sorts of trade secrets to YouTube, we are literally screaming to the world: "ESHETICIANS ARE NOT

NECESSARY IN THE SKIN CARE EQUATION!" And in that case, what is the point of having a facial? Anyone can do it at home because we've taught them online everything they need to know.

It is a puzzle to me why anyone would go all the way through Esthetician school (which is not cheap!) and then bypass their training and knowledge and work as a salesperson, selling products directly to the public.

Some people create their own storms...
and then get mad when it rains.

Referring to Outside Sources

I want to tell you a story about a spa I consulted with a few years ago whose esthetics department was struggling. The spa owner was not a licensed Esthetician and therefore had no hands-on experience in the treatment room. The Spa Director had a massage background, but her experience was at a hotel rather than a spa.

Prior to meeting with management, I first asked to meet with the spa's Estheticians. In that meeting, I discovered that the skin care product line they were using and selling in their spa was one wherein the manufacturer's rep had successfully wined and dined the spa owner (who had no hands-on experience in esthetics) at a trade show which was geared to spa owners and spa managers. This meant that nobody with any direct hands-on experience in esthetics was included in the selection of the product line. For good reason, the Estheticians were not happy.

When I met with management later that day after having talked to the Estheticians, the owner explained to me that when the spa's clientele had a question about products, the clients were advised to call the skin care manufacturer directly or contact them online to get their questions answered. The spa owner was very proud of that protocol and obviously believed the spa was providing good customer service to their clients.

But do you see the problem with this strategy? The Estheticians working in her spa had been cut entirely out of the loop -- they were neutralized, as were potential profitable sales of home care products. This spa owner was literally sending money out of her own door, away from the Estheticians who worked for her, and directly into the shopping cart at the skin care manufacturer's e-store. This spa was literally giving away retail income, as well as losing potential lucrative repeat clients.

UNDER-TRAINED, OVER-PROMISING, NOT WITHIN SCOPE OF LICENSE

If an Esthetician is going to offer a service, he or she must be properly trained to perform that service. This is a safety issue. Clients have a right <u>not</u> to be harmed, as well as a right to expect that they will be receiving what is promised. Here's a list of common issues that can happen due to improper training or carelessness.

- Clients are being harmed
- A client's legal right to <u>not</u> be harmed is being denied
- Dangerous chemicals are being used on or near clients
- Sanitation practices are poor such as improper cleaning and improper storage, which can result in infections
- Contraindications are being overlooked or ignored
- Wax burns, peel burns. (These happen all the time. This is the reason a detailed intake is important, as well as the use of consent forms.)

No intake process. Decades ago, when esthetics was more of a "fluff & puff" service, perhaps a detailed intake process was less essential. However, things have changed.

- Today's skin care products are more active than they used to be.
- These days, clients are partaking in injectables more than ever which means that an Esthetician may have to modify their service to accommodate recent injection sites.

- We use more electrical equipment than we used to which may require additional documentation of contraindications.

ELEVATING TITLE OF LICENSE

"Self-titling" means calling yourself by something that is not officially listed on your state license. For example, at this writing, there is no state in the United States that offers a license such as "Clinical Esthetician" or "Medical Esthetician." Yet you will see Estheticians refer to themselves this way all the time. You will see it on their business cards, their social media pages, and you will see it displayed prominently on their website.

Even more pervasive than "Clinical Esthetician" or "Medical Esthetician" is "Master Esthetician." At this writing, there are only a few states that offer the "Master Esthetician" license. Therefore, only Estheticians in those states who hold a state-issued "Master Esthetician" license are legally permitted to use that title. However, others just simply decide on their own to elevate their title, and by doing so are manipulating consumers. This egregious behavior continues to severely damage the reputation of Estheticians everywhere.

To give you an example of why this matters, let's say a potential client has been referred to two Estheticians::

> **Scenario #1:** Esthetician #1 has been licensed only one year, yet she is illegally identifying herself on her website, on social media, on her business cards, etc. as a "Master Esthetician" even though she didn't earn, and doesn't hold, that license or title.

> **Scenario #2:** Esthetician #2 has been licensed and working in the treatment room for 20 years, and she two has decades worth of post-graduate training and experience. She is following the laws of her state and calls herself exactly what is written on her state license, such as "Esthetician."

The problem: A potential new client has been referred to both of these Estheticians. Odds are, not knowing any better, this potential client will incorrectly be impressed by the fake title of "Master Esthetician" claimed by Esthetician #1. However, in actuality, Esthetician #2 has the most experience, training and education and would be the better choice, if for no other reason than Esthetician #1 is misrepresenting herself and Esthetician #2 is being honest.

It is just not right to mislead clients. We are licensed for a reason. It is law.

If you have extra training or certification in something, by all means you should promote it, but just do it legally. For example, you can very easily (and legally) call yourself a "Licensed Esthetician specializing in Medical Esthetics" or Clinical Esthetics, or whatever your training may be. But self-titling is false advertising, and it is illegal.

LACK OF EDUCATION

There are specific elements that set us apart from all others in the world of skin care. Esthetics evolves continually, so as long as we are working hands-on with clients, it is our responsibility to keep up with all of it. This is why continuing education should be a huge priority throughout an Esthetician's career.

In my opinion, no matter what your specialty might be, these are the basic categories that we should always focus on:

- Safety
- Skin analysis
- Skin conditions
- Understanding ingredients
- Knowing your products
- Prioritizing home care

SOCIAL MEDIA CONS AND PROS

Cons. You have heard me say earlier (and repeatedly) how important it is to "qualify your advisors." Unfortunately, that is hard to do on social media because those platforms are full of people you do not know and cannot see. There are Estheticians from other states, with different training requirements, different rules, and different regulations mandated by their license. There are Estheticians who want to sell you something...maybe it's a class, a product line, a piece of equipment, attendance at an event, or membership in something.

And then there's YouTube, where Estheticians and skin care companies have uploaded many of our trade secrets for the entire world to see. This is extremely detrimental to Professional Estheticians because these videos are showing viewers how not to need Estheticians by training them how to do everything at home.

Additionally, these videos are effectively training MLM companies and other skin care salespeople how to compete with us. We are basically handing non-licensed people a script which contains our terminology, consultation ideas and DIY skin care. So, Estheticians, if you are guilty of this, then no complaining about MLMers trespassing into our territory. because we have provided them with instructions, a script and a road map....so whose fault is it really?

Pros. Personally, I think it's a great idea to belong to private social media groups operated by manufacturers of products or equipment that you are using in your treatment room because there you know you will receive legit information that you can rely on.

It is also a great idea to follow social media sites belonging to your state's licensing board. And I highly recommend you follow your state's NCEA Facebook page. (More about NCEA's important work on behalf of Estheticians in a later chapter.)

Of course, the social aspect of social media can be super fun, but I am simply suggesting that you are very careful about accepting advice that may negatively impact your esthetics career or quash your dreams. Always keep in mind that we do not want our clients to get the majority of their skin care related information online, so we shouldn't either.

4 THE CLIENT

CLIENTS EXPECTATIONS ARE LOW

It is the sad truth that customer service has dropped to an all-time low. Consumers have gotten used to being ignored and disrespected when it comes to customer service. But, on the other hand, there is a way to turn lemons into lemonade here. Because when you do it right, it becomes an opportunity for you to shine.

In this business, you must have great esthetics skills, of course. But this is about customer service beyond the realm of skin care. You have only one chance to make a first impression, so put some thought into it and make it fabulous.

I am going to give you two examples of bad customer service, and I'd like you to consider which one of these options you would choose. I'm going to start with the one that is NOT about esthetics. You've probably been in this situation, and it may never have been on your "bad customer service" radar. But I think you will see the missed opportunity to provide stellar customer service to customers.

Scenario #1 (the wrong way): Say you are in a clothing store and you have seven items you want to try on, but the maximum number of items you're allowed to take with you into the dressing room is six. This means you are required to hand over the extra item to whomever is monitoring the dressing room when you enter.

Once you have tried on the six items that you took into the dressing room and are ready for the remaining item, you look for somebody to hand you your extra item but nobody is available. At that point you have a few options:

1. You can wait inside your dressing room until hopefully somebody comes back into the area and can help you.
2. You can get dressed and step out of the dressing room to find somebody to help you.
3. If you can see the item -- and more importantly have access to it -- you can exit the dressing room and grab it yourself.

Keep in mind though, options 1 and 2 may require you to leave your purse or other valuables unattended while you exit the dressing room, so those options could be risky and therefore unappealing.

And last but not least, Option no. 4 is an obvious one and certainly has been my choice frequently.

4. You can just say "forget it," get dressed, and leave the store.

To be honest, none of these options are ideal. They are inconvenient, they are disrespectful on the part of the store, and the feeling you are left with about the store is frustration and negativity. This is a perfect example of bad customer service and a client not feeling cared for.

Scenario #2 (the correct way). Now let's imagine that same scenario but with a different twist. You are in a different store, and you take your six items to the dressing room. Before you go in, the attendant takes the extra item from you and assures you that he or she will be nearby and ready to hand you your extra item when you are ready for it.

Imagine that even before you are ready for your last item, you hear a soft knock on the dressing room door and a nice voice asks you if you need anything. Perhaps they offer to grab a different size for you, or they ask if you are ready for your extra item.

Whether or not you purchase something that day, you will leave that store having had a positive experience and with a feeling that the store cares. Odds are that you will return to that store and purchase something in the future. Clients have choices, and if a client has a good experience which results in a positive emotional response, they are much more likely to come back again and again.

Scenario #3 (Esthetics): Now I am going to give you example of bad customer service which is very common in the esthetics business. I am sure you have seen ads offering first-time clients something like 10 percent off their first facial? Imagine being a long-time client of this Esthetician or spa who comes in for regular monthly facials and has done so for many years. As a reward for this client's long-term loyalty, they are required to pay full price for something that a brand new client -- who may never return – is charged a lesser price. Do you see the problem here?

These examples may seem mild to you – not necessarily fatal flaws -- but in our business, which is based upon relationships, these things matter. Great customer service must be an ongoing effort. If you make customers feel good, they will stick with you. They will want to spend more time and more money with you, and they will tell their friends about you.

THE BASICS

Clients are pretty simple. They do not ask a lot of us, and we should be honored that that they come back time and time again for our services. But too many Estheticians fall short of meeting the client's basic needs, such as:

- A warm welcome and friendliness
- Respect
- Our full attention while they are in our space
- To feel valued and important
- To be sincerely thanked for their business
- To be invited to return

- To be remembered, even in their absence
- To be appreciated
- To have a good experience with us

The client's experience while they are in our space is not only about facials and skin care. Those meet the clients' <u>external</u> needs, but it is their <u>internal</u> needs that matter most. It is about feeling welcomed, respected, and having our full attention while they are in our space.

Simple things like being sincerely thanked and feeling appreciated will go a long way to establishing a solid, loyal, clientele.

TO BE SINCERELY THANKED

A client is a gift. We need to keep that in mind as we make decisions about how to treat them.

These people can go anywhere for esthetic services. These days there are spas and skin care services on nearly every corner and all over the internet. But your clients choose you…repeatedly. This is a huge compliment and deserves a "Thank you so much. It's always so good to see you, and I'm looking forward to seeing you next month. Please let me know if you have any questions or need anything. Just give me a call and I'll get right back to you. Here's my card."

To be sincerely thanked feels so good to everyone. Unfortunately, it is not a common occurrence these days. Let's bring it back.

I am not suggesting you must sit down and write a note every time there is something to thank them for. A phone call, text or email is perfectly fine. However, for special occasions, there is nothing more personal and impressive than a handwritten note.

I can tell you from personal experience that a handwritten thank you is very special. Throughout the many years I have been in the esthetics business, whether I am training or consulting, occasionally I get a handwritten thank you note. I swear to you, I have saved every one of those handwritten notes. It means so much that somebody took the extra time to write the note and mail it to me.

The reason a simple thank you is so meaningful is simply because it's rare. Mothers do not necessarily get thanked by their kids for all the wonderful things they do, and employers do not always remember to thank employees for their hard work. So any kind of sincere thank you means a lot, and it is so easy to do.

TO BE REMEMBERED

Keeping in touch. There are many ways to keep in touch with your clients on special occasions throughout the year. The customary method is by way of a birthday card. Personally, I think that is okay, but it is just not all that special. Keep in mind that clients get those cards from many other companies, from car dealers to dry cleaners to airlines.

I suggest you do unexpected things so you will stand out from the rest. After all, our relationship with our clients is a personal one, and once a year we can afford to spend a little more time and money on our loyal clients. So, while it is nice for them to know that you care just as much as their local pizza place, it would mean a lot more if you went a little further to show your gratitude.

Take a moment and think about your annual profit on just one of your loyal monthly clients. Don't you think it is worth sending a $25 floral arrangement once per year on her birthday? Or when she is coming in to see you any time around the date of her birthday, have a flower and a card lying on the facial bed when she arrives. Or maybe surprise her with a decadent piece of candy or birthday cookie.

Consider wrapping up a new product or gift item (something she has not previously purchased from you) and give that to her as a birthday gift. It will be impactful, and at your wholesale price, it's a bargain. An extra added bonus: You have just introduced her to a product she may want to purchase in the future.

Every Esthetician working today is providing facial services, but if you can master the art of great customer service, you hold the key to an enormously successful esthetics career.

OUR FULL ATTENTION

Client comfort. Giving clients our full attention while they are in our space means things like checking in regarding their comfort level. Is the facial bed comfortable? How about the temperature of hot towels we may be using?

The last thing we want is for our clients to feel uncomfortable (especially new clients), so we must be certain to avoid creating or adding to a client's discomfort or embarrassment. A client may not mention his or her discomfort, so we must attempt to anticipate it, or at least inquire at the appropriate time.

Explanation and preparation. During a treatment, it is essential to explain to the client what is happening or about to happen. For example, you might say "First, I'm going to exfoliate you, then I'm going to place a warm steam towel on your face, and then I'm going to follow that with a mask." If you are going to use a piece of electrical equipment, then you might say something like: "You're going to hear a buzzing noise, and you're going to feel something cool." It is essential that we offer this information, especially to new clients who have not been with us previously.

To leave or not to leave. A hotly-debated topic these days is whether or not to leave the treatment room while your client is enjoying a lengthy mask. Obviously, you must know the laws of your state on this topic, but my personal opinion is that if you are able to leave the room in a way that allows you to safely monitor your client, then I think leaving is acceptable.

In my solo practice, I used battery-operated tealights so there was nothing that could fall over and burn or harm the client in any way. But I would never leave a client under steam. My office was so close

– and the door separating it from the treatment room so thin – that any noise on the other side of the door would be heard by me, including if they called out to me.

The way I solved the "to leave or not to leave" dilemma is that I asked my clients how they felt about this issue. And what I found was that most of my clients preferred – in fact, loved -- the 20-minute mask time with full darkness and relaxing spa music. What they loved the most was having that 15-20 minute period when nobody was touching them, talking to them, no kids were calling to them. For many, that was their favorite part of the facial experience.

So "to leave or not to leave" is a personal preference, as long as you adhere to the laws mandated by your state, and that the safety of your client is always your number one priority.

PERSONAL DEVELOPMENT TOOL #5
Self-Assessment

How would you grade yourself in each of these subjects? If you are not yet an A+ student, the good news is that it is easy to improve. Put some thought into each of these items and see if you can figure out where there might be room for improvement.

1. How do you greet your clients when they arrive? A handshake? A nod? Maybe a "Hey, there!" There is no right or wrong way, but we always need to be aware of how best to make each client feel welcome and comfortable when they are in our space.
2. Do you regularly check in with your client's level of comfort during a facial as to temperature of the room, the facial bed, the steam towels, or the hot wax? Are you good at sensing when it is time to stop the chit-chat during a treatment and encourage restful silence?

3. Do you take notes during each facial so that you can check in with the client at his or her next appointment regarding likes, dislikes, and results from the previous facial? Do you remember to ask how the products are working for him or her at home? Do you advise your clients when it is time to adjust something due to a shift in the weather or a change in the condition of their skin?

4. Do you sincerely thank your clients whenever the occasion arises? A text, an email, a handwritten note?

5. Do you communicate with clients other than during their appointments? In other words, do you regularly keep in touch?

Clients don't typically leave for financial reasons.
They leave because their needs were not met.

CLIENT DEVELOPMENT

If you have been in the esthetics business for over a year and are still looking for new clients, something is definitely wrong. Odds are that you – like most Estheticians and spas – do not have a Client Development Plan in place.

Looking for new clients
without having a Client Development Plan in place...
is like buying your dream car without first learning how to drive.

Getting people in the door is easy. Just put the word "FREE" on your front door and they will come. However, creating long-term loyal clients is not about simply getting bodies in the door. Success in the esthetics business is built around the relationship those bodies have with you.

A Client Development Plan ("CDP") is something that starts even before the client walks in the door, and it is what keeps them coming back repeatedly. Without a CDP, you are no different than a hamster on a wheel, going round and round. It may keep you busy, but financial success will always be out of reach. Here is a visual that will drive this point home for you: I call it "The Bucket of Rocks."

THE BUCKET OF ROCKS

In this scenario, let's say the esthetics business is the bucket and clients are the rocks. Your bucket has holes in it, which allows the rocks to fall through. In that case, here are your two options:

1. Continually search for new rocks in an attempt to keep the bucket full.

2. Plug the holes in the bucket and keep the rocks you already have.

Success in the esthetics business is not built upon the constant pursuit of new clients. It is based upon client retention. It is about first-time clients becoming long-term repeat clients. It is about customer service, and it is about client care.

In other words, it is about offering clients a great experience, which evokes a positive emotional response. That repeated emotional response results in an experience that clients are drawn to, are willing to pay for, and want to repeat month after month.

There is a very important distinction between a <u>satisfied</u> client and a <u>loyal</u> client. A loyal client is of much higher value. That's because client satisfaction represents an attitude regarding products, services and brands. Whereas client loyalty is about behavior, which translates to "client retention."

As to the clients you already have, remember this: You do not own these clients. They are only temporarily parked on your doorstep and will be glad to move along when they find something better. Therefore, your goal should be to make yourself indispensable to your clients.

THE "CDP"

The subchapters that follow will lay out for you the elements of an effective Client Development Plan:

New Clients v. Former Clients. If you are just starting out in the spa business, of course new clients are a necessity. However, for the rest of you, know this: It is 10-12 times more expensive to bring in one new client than it is to keep the clients you already have. Yet the most common question that is asked of me by working Estheticians is about how to attract more clients.

Far too rare are the business owners who focus on how to keep their current clients loyal and happy. Part of that focus involves making an effort to determine why former clients have gone M.I.A. The reason this element is often overlooked is because, contrary to popular belief, spa owners and solo Estheticians do not really understand that in our business, success is not built on selling treatments and products. I will repeat: Success in our business is built on relationships. Failure to realize this important distinction means that you can send unsolicited emails and hand out business cards all you want, but the end result will not likely be the esthetics career of your dreams.

THE KEY

Let's discuss the Client Relationship, because it is the Holy Grail of the esthetics business; it is the Fountain-of-Youth, the path to success, and it is the key that unlocks the door to esthetics nirvana.

We must wholeheartedly embrace the fact that our business differs from almost every other business out there. As I mentioned earlier, we are in an intimate business wherein we ask women to remove most of their clothing and get into what looks a lot like a bed. And even worse, we then remove their makeup and stare at them through a magnifying lamp. Could it be more distressing for the client?

With that in mind, you can understand why our number one priority should be the relationship we have with our clients. It is at least as important -- more important, I think -- as our skills in the treatment room and the products we sell.

Why do clients go Missing in Action...why do clients leave? It's probably not what you think. Clients leaving an Esthetician is rarely for financial reasons. It actually has more to do with the difference between what they were expecting when they came in as compared to what they actually received. So loyalizing your clients is essential for your financial success.

(I should clarify that "loyalizing" is not an actual word. It is a word that I made up, but what it means is getting new clients in the door and then converting them to long-term loyal clients who come back to you month after month, year after year.)

Another bonus of having a solid bond with your clients is they will forgive you just about anything; for example, if an occasion arises wherein you must reschedule their appointment, or if you do not have one of their products in stock. They will forgive you for that because the bond supports the relationship you have with your clients.

A client will forgive just about anything, if you have a solid bond.

THE CLIENT RELATIONSHIP

Know your Products. A client will be comforted by your passion and knowledge about the products you are using on him or her. Most clients do not care so much about specific ingredients and names of products. What they want to know is: "What will it do for me?" Therefore, product knowledge training for Estheticians is crucial.

This is a common mistake made by spa owners and managers. They do not realize that sending their Estheticians for product training on every product they are expected to use and sell is extremely beneficial for the spa's profit margin. This education is a make-or-break investment in the success of the spa.

The Skin Care Magnet. If you want to mesmerize a potential new client quickly, easily and inexpensively and have her immediately submit to your wisdom and expertise, just put her in a skin scanner!

There are fancy and expensive skin scanners out there but for purposes of this discussion, I am referring to the very basic and affordable version that is similar to a Wood's Lamp encased in a plastic box. It has a window on the outside and a mirror on the inside, and the Esthetician peers through the window while the client views her UV'd reflection in the mirror.

There are photo-technology options such as the high resolution, hand-held microscope that hooks up to your PC, tablet or Smartphone. With this system, you place the hand-held tool on the client's skin and the magnified image appears on the screen. A version of this system also allows for capturing and saving digital photographs that you can keep in your client's digital file for future reference so you can track improvement.

These are very powerful esthetic tools for many reasons. Most importantly, the Esthetician has an opening with which to explain the various conditions that are made visible by the skin scanner such as sun damaged areas, skin in need of exfoliation, oily areas, etc. This is a wonderful opportunity for the Esthetician to suggest and explain various treatments and home care products.

GROUPON

Groupon is one of many collective buying sites that have found their way into esthetics, and they can be hard for most small businesses to resist. By offering deep discounts, these sites offer the potential to attract big numbers of clients and sales. But is it a good idea for your business? When considering this question, please keep in mind that Groupon built its business by working for consumers as opposed to working for small businesses.

The most important component in considering whether to jump on the Groupon bandwagon is whether or not that marketing strategy has the potential to develop long-term repeat clients, which we all know is the real "bread and butter" in our business. Typically, the Groupon shopper's main goal is to find a good deal because he or she does not want to pay full price. Therefore, these people are unlikely to become repeat clients unless you continue to offer the same deep discounts.

Also consider the effect on your current long-term clients. Despite their continued loyalty to you, these loyal clients are required to pay full price for your services while the Groupon shopper receives the same service at a discounted rate. As mentioned in an earlier chapter, this definitely falls into the "bad customer service" category.

Basically, Groupon is just an advertisement disguised as a coupon with a temporary shelf life. And once the coupon no longer exists, the customer's interest disappears as well.

DISCOUNTS AND FREEBIES

Personally, I am not a fan of discounts. Statistically speaking, you will only attract people who are looking for a deal, and when the discount is gone so will those clients be. I suggest leaving discounts to those in the business of food service and car washes, etc.

On the other hand, freebies can work well, but only if you use this strategy wisely. By this, I mean giving away something that costs you very little, such as a sample product or an a la carte service. Here are a few examples:

Free service with a facial. Perhaps offer a free brow or lip hair removal service with a specific facial treatment for a precise period of time. The reason this is a great strategy is because it is an opportunity to introduce your hair removal services to your facial clients, which may result in lots of additional income from waxing or sugaring.

You can also reverse this strategy and offer a free facial with lip/brow/chin hair removal which might result in your hair removal clients having their very first facial and becoming repeat facial clients. In other words, these are wonderful strategies that will introduce services that your existing clients have not yet tried.

Free product. The same thing works with free product. If you have recently brought a new product into your lineup, you can introduce your clients by giving them a sample or travel size version. And for your top-level clients, you may want to give them a full-size product.

Just be sure to give them something that they are not already using, because the goal is to introduce them to something new which ultimately they will want to purchase in the future.

Free Introductory Consultation and Skin Evaluation. This is such a great way to get potential clients into your business, but of course, it's what you do once they are in the door that will determine if they become a loyal client. For that reason, this evaluation should be just long enough and detailed enough to introduce yourself, your spa or esthetics business, and your menu. In other words, save your detailed consultation for paying customers or first-time facial clients.

BEHIND THE SCENES: A Note for Spa Owners

A common fear among spa owners is that if you provide your Estheticians with training, someday they may leave your spa and take your clients with them. While that is a legitimate concern, it is not an insurmountable one. Spa owners and managers must also make an effort to create a solid bond between the client and the spa. This will ensure that the client will choose to stay with the spa even if his or her regular Esthetician is no longer there.

The best way for a spa to create a loyal bond is simply to show their clients that they care. This starts with stellar customer service offered by the owner, manager, front desk and all other employees that clients encounter before and after they step into the treatment room. A warm "hello" and a "thank you" goes a long way.

Other important factors regarding whether a client sticks with the spa or leaves with the Esthetician are the location of the spa, easy parking, convenient hours of operation and personal service whenever possible. This means not relying exclusively on online booking and social media for interaction with clients and potential clients.

BE THE CLIENT

ASSESS YOUR TREATMENT ROOM OR SPA

It is crucial to regularly assess your facility, as if you were the client. This is the only way you can ever really know what your client's experience will be. This sounds like a no-brainer, but as vital as this component may be, it is rarely considered.

You must periodically remove your Esthetician hat and become the client for 15 minutes. Experience things as your client would. For example, what does the client see and feel in some of these places:

Treatment room:

- Lay on the facial bed. How does it feel? Is it comfortable or does something need to be adjusted?
- Look up at the ceiling. Does your client see stained ceiling tiles or dirty fan blades?
- Look side-to-side. Is there trash, dirty towels, storage items or cleaning supplies visible?
- Look down. Are there stains on the carpet or wax on the floor?
- Look at the walls and any accessories. Are they dirty, dusty, or worn out?
- How about sheets and towels? Are they worn out, dingey or stained?
- Check the wax pot. Is it messy?

Waiting room/Front desk:

- Where does your client sit while she is waiting? What is in her line of sight? Trash, dust, stains?

- What does she hear? (Hopefully it's not your receptionist talking to a friend about personal issues.)
- Your front desk should be a thing of beauty. It must be clean, uncluttered, and easy for the client to utilize when purchasing product, making a payment, and scheduling an appointment.

Bathroom:

Cleanliness in the bathroom is critical because it reflects everything about you and your business.

- Is the trash bin enclosed or are the contents visible? Is there an odor emanating from the trash bin?
- How about feminine hygiene products, combs and brushes, and cleaning supplies? Are they visible?
- Are there plenty of paper towels and extra toilet paper available?
- Is there dust on the wall art, fake flowers or plants?

If you don't have enough cupboard space to get these items out of view, invest in some inexpensive baskets or decorative boxes and stack them.

Retail area:

A common problem are dusty shelves.

- Is your retail area clean?
- Are the shelves and products dusty?
- Is your signage legible?

I know it can be difficult to stay on top of dusty shelves, but you must find a way. At the very least, keep a feather duster handy to be used between regular cleaning of the shelves. Dust becomes visible when a product is removed from the shelf, so keep an eye on that.

This is a task that should be assigned to staff and completed on a regularly scheduled basis as opposed to "as-needed," because "as-needed" can be interpreted many different ways.

CLIENT'S INTERACTION WITH STAFF

You must assess everything and everyone your clients will encounter while they are in your space, and that includes your staff.

Odors: Employees. You need to double-check for any odors, even perfume if that is one of your rules. I was not a big fan of perfume in my space because it competed with the lovely scents of my essential oils. You also must consider that some clients may be allergic to synthetic fragrances.

Attire: Check employees' attire from top to bottom. Assess their clothing choices, their footwear, hands, and feet too if visible. You may decide it is time to institute a footwear rule such as closed toe only.

Work habits: Cleanliness in and out of the treatment room matters enormously. And do the people who work for you behave like team players, and do they get along with other staff members and clients?

Smoking: Even if your employees are not smoking inside your space, sometimes that odor follows them back inside.

Mystery Shop. You should "mystery shop" your front desk. Borrow a friend whose voice will not be recognized and listen in as he or she calls in to make an appointment (which you can cancel later) or to ask questions.

The same thing goes with online scheduling. Take yourself through the process so you can assess how it is working and what the client's experience is. It is imperative that you are aware of anyone or anything that may need improvement because in most cases, this will be the first contact a potential client has with your business. This is a make-or-break moment and it is crucial.

When you hire new Estheticians, have them take you through a client consultation so you can see everything they do from beginning to end. That way, you can assess if it is the way you want it to be. My opinion is that you should train everybody yourself (including your existing Estheticians) so everything will be done uniformly and according to your standards. Prepare forms for them to use and give them printed rules and step-by-step directions that they can rely on until they are performing according to your standards.

YOUR CREDENTIALS

Rather than filling up the walls in your treatment room with art and accessories, use that precious real estate to further the bond with your clients and gain their trust. My suggestion is that you frame your Continuing Education certificates and hang them on your treatment room wall. There is nothing more comforting for a new client who might be feeling a little intimidated as she reclines in the facial chair, than glancing around your treatment room and seeing evidence of your esthetics training, ability and experience.

Make the display as artsy or clinical as you wish, to reflect your personality and work environment. Just don't waste that valuable wall space!

THE KINDERGARTNER

Even though a new client may have had a facial treatment elsewhere at some point in her life, it's essential to make her comfortable from the very beginning of her relationship with you. I use the reference "kindergartner" to describe how a first-time client should be treated because it is rather similar to taking a kindergartner to school for the first time. Just like an Esthetician's new client, these newcomers do not yet know the ropes.

They are not sure where to sit, where to put their stuff or where the bathroom is. There is so much they do not yet know, and you never want to make a first-time client feel uncomfortable or confused in your space. It is up to us to remove all those potential obstacles.

For example, indicate not just with your words but also with a gesture so she understands exactly where her clothes, shoes, and accessories are to be placed once she has removed them. Be specific as to which items of clothing she must remove, and which items are optional.

Hand the facial wrap to her (or place it on the facial bed…whatever your protocol may be) only after indicating how it should be worn. Do not simply tell her. Instead, hold the facial wrap up to your own body and demonstrate how high it goes, how to fasten it, etc.

Pull the sheets back on the facial table so she understands she is to get under the sheets -- and be sure to mention face up. I know that sounds like a no-brainer, but you would be surprised at the stories I have heard!

Once the client has settled into the facial bed, check her comfort level, and take a moment to outline how things will go during the service. For example, you can say "First, I am going to go through the intake process and ask you some questions, and then I'm going to cleanse your face, my mag light will be next…"

In other words, err on the side of over-informing your first-time clients. We do not want a first-time client to experience any sort of discomfort. Causing a new client to feel inept or embarrassed can be a fatal flaw in the development of a fledgling client relationship.

The first time a client walks into your business,
a relationship has begun.

There are several components to the client bond, and they probably are not what you think. Once you understand this important aspect of the esthetics business, it is relatively easy to accomplish. At the very heart of it, the client bond is like a beautiful flower; first you plant it, but if you do not properly tend to it, it will die.

LISTEN TO THEIR STORY

I know our job is to assess skin conditions and offer solutions, but do not forget to take some time to get to know your client. You have a semi-naked woman without makeup in your facial chair, so if she wants to elaborate on something during the intake process, just listen. Let her tell you about her current skin condition, product usage, facial history, etc. And be sure to note any important information that comes out of that conversation because, trust me, during an intake procedure done properly, a lot of information will come out that was not included on the form.

If you create a strong bond in the beginning, you will have a loyal client for years…and then it will be your turn to talk.

One Good Thing

Of course, your primary job is to identify and resolve any issues with your client's skin and home care habits, but somewhere in all of that, the client can feel burdened with the diagnosis. They hear a lot of "this is not right" or "we can improve that" from us.

If you can leave your client with one (even very small) word of praise, do it. Something like "I can tell you take very good care of your skin" or "I'm glad you are interested in skin care." It's a gift that she needs and will not soon forget.

When you see something beautiful in someone, tell them.
It may take only seconds to say but for them, it could last a lifetime.

REPORT CARD

This is something I came up with one year after opening my spa. It was kind of a one-year anniversary report card. As I mentioned earlier, I was new at the spa thing, so I wanted feedback and I was not afraid to hear it. I know it sounded like a survey, but I didn't want to call it that because we all get so many surveys. So, I called it a Report Card. Here are a few of the questions I asked my clients:

- Which services have you had at our spa?
- Which service was your favorite (and why)?
- Which service was your least favorite (and why)?
- Is there anything you think we could do better?
- Are there any services you wish we had on our menu?
- Do you enjoy our newsletter?

To get the most out of this strategy, it is wise to invest in the cost of a return stamped envelope, and let the recipients know that they can participate anonymously. If you are paying for the envelope to be returned and you are not asking them to provide their name, you will get the most honest replies. The information that comes from this strategy can be extremely helpful, and it will assist you in defining the direction of your esthetics business going forward.

Just remember that you do not have to be all things to all people. You will always be happiest when you are doing the things you love, and those are the things you will be best at. Once you find out from your clients which services they prefer, or you learn of any improvements they might suggest, you will then be able to adjust your menu which will increase bookings and ultimately increase profit.

EDUCATE

For you. There are many reasons Estheticians must keep themselves educated and keep up with esthetics trends, which change all the time. Education must be ongoing, year after year, because the more you know, the more you can share with your clients. Clients are much more sophisticated today than they were when I became an Esthetician, and that's a good thing. However, on the other hand, a lot of the information clients are getting their hands on is wrong.

For clients. Estheticians must know the skin very well so they can explain it to clients and also use visuals to maximize a client's understanding of their skin. We want clients to look to us for skin care info. We don't want them to get it online. So, the more you educate your clients, the more they will trust you and depend on you. And that's how you create an unshakeable bond and loyal, long-term clients.

It always seems impossible...until it's done.
~Nelson Mandela

5 THE FORMULA

There really is a formula for success in the spa business and I'm going to tell you what it is. It's pretty simple, there are only 5 steps. However, if any one of these steps is faulty or missing, it is impossible to build and maintain a financially successful esthetics business.

The 5-step Formula consists of:

1. The Esthetician
2. The Product Line
3. The Menu
4. The Intake Process
5. The Home Care Products

FORMULA STEP 1: The Esthetician

Training: Estheticians are the hub of any esthetic department obviously. Therefore, they must be properly trained.

- Estheticians must receive product knowledge training for all product lines they are using and selling. They must know everything they can about each product being used on a client, such as how it works, how to store it, what is in it, what it is supposed to do, any possible contraindications, and what could go wrong.

- Estheticians must be well-trained and competent in the usage of any equipment being used on a client.
- Estheticians who work in a spa environment with transient clientele must have especially good people skills, primarily with regard to women.

You will notice that the act of giving a facial or the specifics of giving a facial are not the priority here. That's because on the list of what makes an esthetics career successful, giving a facial is not at the top. What matters most is understanding why you are giving the facial, which facial is best for that client, and which products are best to use on that client. These variables change constantly due to the client's ever-evolving skin condition, so continuing education is a priority as long as you are a working Esthetician.

Rules and Laws: Estheticians who are working hands-on with clients must be well-versed in every rule and law under which they are licensed:

- Client safety is the priority. That is the rule. When an Esthetician harms a client, it hurts all of us and it puts our license at risk.
- Estheticians must know their state's rules and regulations and must stay within them at all times. Too often, Estheticians do not know the rules and regulations of their state, and that can -- and often does -- lead to mistakes and injuries.

FORMULA STEP 2: Products

Product Line. An essential element to an Esthetician's success is choosing the perfect product line. And by "perfect," I mean: Fits the goals of your esthetics business, and most importantly, produces the visible results that your clientele is looking for.

There are also many considerations we should keep in mind when selecting a vendor that go well beyond the products. Here is my list of priorities:

- Great customer service and support
- Website with professional-only area
- Low minimum reorder requirement
- Easy shipping
- Exhibits at our trade shows
- Offers Product Knowledge training
- Fits the business's goals and image
- Packaging
- Social media closed/private group

Service/Support. The first one on my list is great customer service and support. To me, this means that if I make a phone call to the vendor or send an email, I would really appreciate a response relatively quickly. It is not my habit to contact a vendor often so when I do, it is for a very good reason and I would like somebody to get back to me quickly.

Website. I prefer a vendor whose website has a "professional only" area, and that is because oftentimes it is not necessary that I talk to directly to anybody. I might just need some quick information. Like maybe I need to view a product's ingredient deck, or perhaps I need to be reminded of the steps in a protocol that I have learned from them. I appreciate easy access to basic information.

Low minimum order requirement. This is especially important for Solo Estheticians because they typically do not have big budgets or an abundance of storage space.

In the esthetics business, it is not unusual to find that opening orders are high for new accounts. However, if a vendor's re-order requirement is high, Estheticians may be forced to add products to their order that they may not even need, simply to meet the vendor's high minimum reorder requirement. In doing that, it may result in products expiring before the Esthetician is able to use them or sell them.

There are plenty of fabulous professional skin care product manufacturers who are supporting Estheticians by keeping their minimum order requirements manageable. And what that means to me is that if they are taking appropriate steps to help my esthetics business, then I will show my gratitude by using and selling their products.

Easy shipping. It is important to me that the distributor is convenient. For example, I am on the west coast. If my products are being shipped from the east coast, it could take a week. And for a Solo Esthetician who does not typically have lots of extra products in stock, I need to depend on quick shipping.

Exhibit at our trade shows. In my long career as an Esthetician, I have carried many skin care product brands, and one of these opted not to exhibit at our professional trade shows. It was from dealing with this company that I realized how much less direct information and training was available from companies who do not exhibit.

Personally, I love going up to a vendor's booth at a trade show, talking to the rep, asking questions, learning about current products, learning about what products are being formulated now and will be available soon. It is important to me to be able to touch the products, smell them, and perhaps see or participate in a demo before I order.

Product Knowledge training. This is essential in order to properly care for our clients. We must understand every detail about the products we use and sell. With the manufacturer's Product Knowledge training, we will learn the protocols that work best with each product.

Of course, there is an abundance of online training available, but because the esthetics business is based on personal relationships, in-person training is better for Estheticians. There are classes to attend at trade shows where you can get hands-on experience that is not possible online.

Fits your business goals and image. This depends upon what esthetics specialty you are focusing on. For example, if you are specializing in acne, you may find that many vendors do not offer specific products and protocols to accommodate that specialty. That means you will have to switch product lines or add a secondary line.

Packaging. Not everyone cares so much about packaging, which is fine, because quite honestly what is inside the package is most important. But packaging does matter. It definitely matters to me. I want the packaging of my product lines to look professional, classy and clean because that is part of the image I want for my business.

Social media closed/private group. Emphasis on the "closed." I think it is great to belong to groups that are run by the manufacturer of any product line or equipment that you are using because it is a great way to get questions answered quickly. But on the flip side, I am not a fan of companies who upload Professional Esthetician facial protocols on public sites.

In other words, I prefer to spend my money with companies who are supporting Estheticians rather than competing with them or neutralizing them.

BACKBAR

Here is the criteria that matters most when I am assessing a manufacturer's back bar options:

Home Use. I do not want all the backbar products to be available in retail size for home use. Of course, there will be some crossover, but when every single product that I use in the treatment room is available for home use, what is the point? I have dropped skin care lines because of this.

Same thing with electrical equipment. If the identical item, same strength, same intensity, is now available in a home care version, I will drop it and move onto something else. Professional Estheticians should stay at least one step ahead of whatever is happening in the world of DIY skin care. This is why trade shows are so important, so you are always in the loop regarding any new professional esthetics equipment options.

Ingredients. Estheticians understand the variables regarding how and where ingredients are sourced, what fillers and additives can cause skin problems, etc. So high-quality ingredients from a reputable company that I trust is key for me.

Fits your client base. Obviously if your client base has certain requirements such as perhaps they want gluten free, organic, or maybe they have oncology limitations, then you must bring in specific products to meet those needs. Not every product line offers products to serve every possible client (nor should they). I prefer smaller manufacturers who specialize.

Expiration and budget. These two are similar in that they are both related to the high minimum order requirements that some companies impose wherein you must meet a minimum monetary requirement, or you are required to meet a minimum unit order. Because backbar products are larger, it may take longer to use them up in the treatment room, which means expiration can become a problem.

When I first started my spa, being the novice that I was, I purchased all six of the back bar cleansers offered to me by the company rep. Fortunately, I figured out pretty quickly that no Esthetician really needs six cleansers. Cleansers go on the skin and they are removed quickly. So with the exception of a few specialty services, a milky cleanser and a cleanser that lathers will do the job for most facial services.

Specialty products. I like to have specialty products that will make my facials different from each other. I prefer to have a lot of serums because you can mix and match and "cocktail" serums (while wearing your Chemist hat!). If your product line offers other specialty treatments or products, such as eye treatments or body products, why not give those a try?

When I was a new Esthetician, I used masks that came in a tube. They were messy and they were not easy to remove. Fortunately, I discovered sheet masks which I can easily peel off my client, and there is no residue that must be removed with water or steam towels. The advantage for the client is that because I have not ended the facial by removing product from their face, the mask ingredients are able continue their penetration deep into the skin even after the client has departed my facial room.

Client safety. I have encountered products that have a short shelf life and have been known to go bad, which may cause the skin to react. Some products with active ingredients sold for home use have also been known to cause a reaction even when they are fresh. These are obvious safety issues. Therefore, a lot of research is required before signing on to a new skin care line.

PRODUCT DIVERSION

Product diversion refers to products that are being sold outside of authorized distribution channels. The popularity of the skin care industry and the evolution of the internet have created a huge problem which targets the online shopper.

The methods of product diversion are varied. Here is one scenario which explains why an Esthetician might be compelled to participate in product diversion:

- A wholesale client (in this case, an Esthetician) uses his or her state license to legally order product from a manufacturer of professional skin care products with an intent to sell them as retail products in his or her esthetics business.
- Because many manufacturers have high minimum order requirements, often the Esthetician is not able to sell the entire inventory to his or her clients before the products become stale or expire.
- At that point, the Esthetician's options are to sell the stale or expired products on eBay or Amazon or off-load the products to a third party. Both options are without the manufacturer's consent.

Other possibilities are more sinister, such as the possibility that the diverted products may have been stolen or could be the result of fraud. Diverted products can be counterfeit, diluted, or altered in some way. There could be fillers added, or the products might be stale or expired. There could even be a completely different product inside the bottle as opposed to what is indicated on the label.

Product diversion is a big problem in esthetics so it is important that Estheticians are clear about what "product diversion" means and can speak eloquently about it to clients and to the general public. Be sure to have something on your website about it because people need to understand that there is a big difference between the quality of products people may be seeing in discount stores or online versus the fresh, well-sourced, well-maintained, properly stored and safely shipped products that a Professional Esthetician offers.

BEHIND THE SCENES: A Note to Spa Owners

It is vital that you involve your Estheticians in the research and selection of skin care products. Skin care lines are not created equal, and if an Esthetician does not know well (and hopefully, love) the products he or she is required to use, the spa's profit will suffer.

I once consulted with a spa whose Spa Director was a massage therapist with a background in hotel management. Maybe this sounds good on paper but in actuality, the spa was suffering. This Spa Director had no specific training, experience or understanding about esthetics equipment, products, ingredients or facial services even though she thought she knew a lot. These are technical skills, all of which require specific training. (This spa has since closed.)

Unfortunately, this is relatively common because owners of spas often incorrectly assume that someone who has worked at a spa in any capacity is qualified to manage the esthetics department. It is simply not true, and that assumption can damage the profitability and reputation of the business. Therefore, it is highly recommended that spa owners or managers incorporate a trained and qualified Esthetician into any important decision-making regarding your esthetics department.

FORMULA STEP 3: The Menu

"Why are Facials Important?"

This is an important question. Do you have an answer for this question? Not only should you be able to answer the question but you should be able to explain in one sentence why facials are important.

Here is an interesting statistic: **Studies show that 60% of people define their skin type and home care incorrectly.**

Isn't that amazing? That's over half! This drives home the point that consumers need a trained and licensed professional to analyze their skin, provide accurate information, create an appropriate treatment plan, and make home care recommendations. That's how people will reach their skin care goals. And that's exactly what Estheticians do.

In an earlier chapter I talked about having a Client Development Plan and now we are going to get very specific regarding how to write your service menu so as to attract new clients. We will take a look at what is in a client's mind when he or she assesses an Esthetician's service menu. I will give you very specific examples of how some Estheticians get it right and how too many get it wrong, followed by how things can be improved.

CREATE YOUR OWN MENU

My advice is that you should not waste money by having a menu professionally printed, especially these days when everybody has a website. But do have a hard copy menu available because there will be uses for that. That can be easily accomplished by creating a menu on your computer on letter-size paper, which will allow you to fold it and mail it when needed.

Because your menu is created on your computer, you can edit it any time you want to. You can add seasonal services, and you can change the color of the paper it is printed on to coincide with a particular season. You can include a flyer announcing an upcoming event or a new service, or a new employee. It keeps things fresh and new and exciting for your clients and for you. And always be sure to keep an updated version of your service menu on your website.

UNCOMPLICATE YOUR MENU

First-Timer Facial

During my Business Essentials 101 class, I would ask the attendees a specific question, and 99% of the time, somebody in the class gets it right. Here is that question:

"When a potential client calls a spa, what question do they always ask?"

The correct answer is: "How much are your facials?"

These potential clients do not ask this question because they really want to know the price. They ask it because they can't think of anything else to say to whomever answers the phone. And what is the typical response from the front desk staff? They give the price of the spa's lowest-priced facial, of course. And that's a problem!

A reception staff that is property trained will know this is a caller's most often-asked question, so they are prepared to engage in conversation with those potential clients. And that's very good!

To make this situation easy on my reception staff and any potential client who calls in, I created what I called the "First-Timer Facial" (FTF). It's not a fancy name, but it serves the important purpose of making it clear to anyone viewing my menu for whom this facial is intended.

The FTF has a set price and a specific amount of time, but the components of the facial are determined when the client arrives and meets with the Esthetician. What this means to the client is that he or she does not have to know his or her skin type or current skin care needs and is not forced to choose a facial from a complicated spa menu.

And for the front desk staff's benefit, there is no need to "sell" a particular facial. The receptionist only needs to know the components of the FTF and be able to explain to the potential client that his or her facial will be determined in conjunction with the Esthetician based upon a detailed consultation and evaluation. After all, it is part of the Esthetician's job to determine which facial treatment is best for our client, right? It's not the responsibility of the client.

With the FTF, the pressure is taken off the client and the front desk, and trust in the Esthetician's expertise, and the bonding process, has already begun.

> ▸ FTF must include at least 15 minutes of pre-facial consultation/chat time and 15 minutes post-facial time for discussion and recommendation of home care products and protocol.

Deciphering our Code

Estheticians have their own unique language which makes perfect sense when we are talking to each other, but it doesn't necessarily make sense to – let's call them "civilians" – those who are not in the esthetics business.

Let's look at a few facial descriptions from the perspective of the client (or prospective client).

The Menu of Services

Below you will see two descriptions from a service menu of a very prestigious spa where I used to live. I have been to this spa so I can vouch for the beautiful facility, lovely treatment rooms, pretty décor, etc. But if you had not been there and were simply judging this spa by its service menu, your first impression would probably be mediocre at best.

I have cut and pasted these two descriptions unedited so you will see the typos in the description of their Blueberry Peel (typos are noted in **bold**) to emphasize how important it is that we proofread our menus, or ask somebody to do it for us if spelling and grammar are not among your many talents.[2]

Of course, flawless spelling is not a requirement to be a great Esthetician. Some of the most brilliant and talented people I know can't spell very well. However, misspellings on a service menu indicates that the Esthetician (or in this case, spa) is careless, and that can be enough to keep potential clients away. It is such an easy thing to catch with spell check, so there really is no excuse not to have a properly written service menu.

▶ **POMEGRANATE PEEL**: Lavish your skin with antioxidants to prevent free radical damage and support the life span of healthy cells. This peel works beautifully to soften and exfoliate your skin, while adding anti-inflammatory and antioxidant protection.

▶ **BLUEBERRY PEEL:** Suitable for all skin types, this refreshing peel exfoliates with Lactic Acid and Vitamin C, then purifies the **skn** with the powerful antioxidant properties of blueberries. The hydrating benefits of D-Glucuronic Acid are the finishing touch to this **wonderfull** gentle, yet effective peel. Although new, this is already one of our most popular treatments to exfoliate, purify, and smooth the skin.

---

[2] *As a court reporter, I learned to read each line from right to left at least once. This method prevents context from getting in the way of spotting misspelled words.*

THE CLIENT'S PERSPECTIVE

Let's break down the elements of the Pomegranate Peel and assess it from a client's perspective. And later you can dissect the Blueberry Peel as if you were the client. (Probably starting with "Will blueberries make my skin turn blue?") I have put in **bold** the words and phrases that could be problematic from the client's perspective as he or she reads this.

Pomegranate Peel:

Lavish your skin with **antioxidants** to prevent **free radical damage** and support the life span of healthy cells. This peel works beautifully to **soften** and **exfoliate** your skin, while adding **anti-inflammatory** and antioxidant protection.

1. **Antioxidants** – A client may know the definition of "antioxidants," but it is doubtful that the typical client understands specifically how antioxidants are related to skin damage and skin care.
2. **Free radical damage** – same as above. It's a complicated process and the general public may not understand the connection to skin care.
3. **Soften** – The descriptive words usually associated with skin care are more along the lines of "tighten" and "firm;" in other words, the opposite of "soften."
4. **Exfoliate** – This is one of the most important words in the esthetic dictionary, however, it is unfamiliar to many consumers.
5. **Anti-inflammatory** – Everyone knows that inflammation is not a good thing, but not everybody understands how it relates to skin damage and skin care.

WHAT'S IN IT FOR ME?

This is the question that most clients have in mind when they are assessing a facial service menu. For that reason, we want to choose our words carefully. We want to use language that a potential client can immediately relate to.

For example, the basic skin types are: Dry, sensitive, normal, combo, oily, acneic. Potential clients will put themselves in one of these categories. When they are then assessing the facial service options, we want to offer descriptive words that will tell them exactly what the benefits will be.

What are the benefits for the potential client? Well, for example, they will be nourished, moisturized, balanced, purified, decongested. These are words potential clients can relate to. For this reason, we must incorporate simple but descriptive words into our facial service menu.

EXAMPLE: Clarify the Benefits.

Below is a much better way to explain the benefits of a facial from the client's perspective. This description is relatable and user-friendly. Once again, I have put in bold all the descriptive words used in the Hydrating Facial description, which as you can see makes this service very easy to understand. It answers the "what's in it for me?" question by providing the what, who, when and why.

This description includes information regarding which client this facial would most benefit, as well as examples of when they may want to have this facial…such as before a party or at a time when their skin is dehydrated from traveling.

As you read this, please keep in mind the potential client's question, "What's in it for me?"

Hydrating Facial:

"There's dry, and then there's really **DRY**. The **easy solution** is the **soothing, super-hydrating** effects of collagen. The **frequent flyer's** best friend, and definitely the facial you want **before a party** or **photos**. You **glow, girl!** (**Recommended for** Baby Boomers, mature, menopausal and dry skin types.)"

Now let's examine the descriptive words in the Hydrating Facial:

1. **Dry** – Everybody knows this word, and it is a very common skin condition that Estheticians are regularly asked to resolve.
2. **Easy solution** – This is self-explanatory, of course. Both of these words feel optimistic and comforting to clients.
3. **Soothing** – Easily recognizable to clients, optimistic, comforting.
4. **Super-hydrating** – The obvious solution to the common dry skin complaint.
5. **Frequent flyer, before a party or photos** – Makes it clear who specifically might benefit from this facial and when.
6. **Glow** – No explanation needed. Who doesn't want to glow after a facial?!
7. **Recommended for Baby Boomers, mature, menopausal and dry skin types** – It's abundantly clear who will benefit most from this facial.

BEHIND THE SCENES: A Note to Spa Owners

Very often women will go for spa services with a friend, and afterward they are very likely to compare their experiences. Therefore, it is crucial that your Estheticians are trained to follow similar protocols for each of the services on your menu. Of course, the Esthetician's personality and style will define each facial, but the basic elements of the service should be uniform.

FORMULA STEP 4: Intake Process

The intake process is extremely important for reasons of client safety, of course, but it is also the place where retail sales begin as the Esthetician discusses with the client his or her skin care goals and current home care regimen.

A huge mistake made by many spas is skipping this vital step with first-time clients. The intake process is where a bond and trust are created between the Esthetician and the client, which then leads to repeat customers and continued retail sales long after the client has exited the esthetic business or spa.

Why Does it Matter?

The intake process is mandatory for any Professional Esthetician. It is not optional. This is the most important part of your esthetics business.

SAFETY is always the priority, of course. However, it is also your opportunity to educate the client. This is how you will determine which service and products are best for your client. Ultimately, it is as a result of the intake process that you will achieve the best results.

NEW CLIENT EVALUATION

- ○ Skin Scanner/Scope
- ○ Manual Evaluation
- ○ Medical History
- ○ Contraindications
- ○ Issues and Goals
- ○ Home Care
- ○ Notes and Records

Skin Scanner. I have already mentioned the skin scanner, also known as a skin scope. If you are familiar with a Woods Lamp, the application is similar. Because of the skin scanner's configuration, the Esthetician can explain to the client exactly what he or she is seeing in real time. And I can tell you from personal experience that it is quite a shock to the client when they are viewing themselves this way for the first time. The good news about this is that following a skin scanner experience, clients will do anything you tell them to!

There is a diagram that often accompanies a skin scanner. This visual is what the client views to help them understand what they're seeing when they are under the UV light of the skin scanner. The skin scanner is a very powerful tool to help clients understand that the Esthetician knows what he or she is talking about. It will also allow the client to trust the Esthetician's judgment and the advice being offered. I highly recommend checking these out next time you attend a trade show. Ask for a demo so you will get the full client (and Esthetician) experience.

It is also a good idea to have other visuals available such as a visual of Fitzpatrick Types or the Glogau scale, or perhaps a moisture checker. Anything you have available that you can share with the client so she or he can experience visually what you are explaining will encourage the client to believe you and rely on you for your skin care knowledge and expertise.

THE INTAKE FORM

I recommend that you create your own Intake Form rather than using one from a manufacturer or one you found online. The form really must be customized to fit your particular clientele and your esthetics business.

As you continue to use your Intake Form, you may find that it changes. Perhaps you will realize you forgot to include something or based upon your specific clientele, there may be a section on the form that you really don't need. Because you have created the Intake Form on your computer, you can edit it as needed.

Most importantly, you must get enough information to ensure your client's safety and protect yourself by making certain you are not overlooking some sort of contraindication. Quite frankly, if I ever went somewhere for a facial and the Esthetician did not have some sort of intake process, I would get off the table, I would walk out, and I would never look back. And for safety reasons, I would tell everybody I knew not to go there for a facial.

You can assess the quality of an Esthetician's training, knowledge, and expertise by way of his or her intake process. So if there is no intake process, well, that's just a huge red flag.

And to be clear, the level of intake process and depth of form varies depending upon the location. For example, a resort spa whose main goal is to offer generic feel-good facials to clients who are on vacation (people they will likely never see again) does not require the same level of detail as would an Esthetician who specializes in clinical esthetics and sees regular clients repeatedly. But no matter the location, some information is always necessary if you are going to be applying products to a client.

Completing the Intake Form. The Intake Form should be filled out with the client as opposed to handing her a form and a pen and asking her to complete the form herself. This important step is so much more than information on a page. This is a huge opportunity to bond with the client as you ask the questions, record the answers, answer questions she may have, and discuss various items and issues during the process. The information you will extract due to the back-and-forth dialog as you go through the Intake Form with your client is the most valuable information you will ever receive.

This is where the bonding process begins as you go through this personal information and allow her to get to know you. It allows her to begin to feel more comfortable and ultimately relax into trusting you. This will allow you to get to know her too, such as her personality, her goals, her fears about aging, her self-image, etc. This is a personal experience for the client who is oftentimes providing private information, and it should be treated respectfully and with great care.

My intake process. My protocol was to pull my chair up next to the client once she was comfortable in the facial bed. I would place my chair such that she did not have to turn her head to look at me. In other words, I made it easy for her.

I had the form on a clipboard, and I would go through the questions in each section one-by-one. It does not matter if the conversation goes off track, off topic, and away from what's contained in the form. Consistent bits of helpful information will result from this process, so be ready to take notes.

The process of filling out the Intake Form with the client is also the first step in laying the foundation for future retail sales. (This will be discussed in more detail when we get to the Home Care portion of the Intake Form.)

ABCDEs of Skin Cancer.

Before we get into the specifics of the Intake Form, I must point out that it is imperative Estheticians are able to identify the various types of moles and know when to refer their client to a reputable dermatologist. Estheticians have a front row seat to things happening with our client's skin so if you see something suspicious, do not panic the client but do recommend that he or she sees a dermatologist ASAP. Also be sure to suggest to your clients that they have an annual mole check (which of course Estheticians should do as well.)

- ○ **A = Asymmetry**
  One half is unlike the other half.
- ○ **B = Border**
  An irregular, scalloped or poorly defined border.

- **C = Color**
  Is varied from one area to another; has shades of tan, brown or black, or is sometimes white, red, or blue.
- **D = Diameter**
  Melanomas are usually greater than 6 mm (the size of a pencil eraser) when diagnosed, but they can be smaller.
- **E = Evolving**
  A mole or skin lesion that looks different from the rest or is changing in size, shape or color.

INTAKE FORM CATEGORIES

Here are some suggestions that you can pick from to use in your Intake Form as they apply to you (I am not suggesting that you need all of these, or that this is a complete list):

Skin Scanner Evaluation:
- Sun damage: Mild, moderate or severe; and location.
- Dehydration: Mild, moderate or severe; and water consumption
- Skin type, Fitzpatrick type, Glogau scale

Manual Evaluation:
This is a list of things you might see as you examine your client's face under a mag lamp. It is important to document anything noteworthy such as large pores or broken capillaries, etc., which will serve as a baseline for future facial appointments.

- Deep wrinkles; location
- Closed comedones; location
- Open comedones; location
- Enlarged pores; location
- Milia; location
- Capillaries; location
- Acne; location and grade
- Lesions; location and cause
- Suspicious moles; location
- Evidence of Rosacea; location

Medical History:
Here are some basic questions for the medical history of the Intake Form. You must tread lightly and carefully when inquiring about personal information such as medications and personal health. And of course, do not advise above your license.

- Previous referral to the dermatologist; reason
- Allergies (aspirin, citrus, sea products, iodine, milk, nuts, latex, etc.)
- Oral or topical medications that may be affecting the client's skin
- Current health conditions that may be affecting the client's skin
- Pregnant or nursing moms
- Hormonal issues, including HRT
- Retin A or Accutane use; when?

Summary:
If you find something unusual, you might need to refer to a dermatologist. Be prepared by doing some research to find a reputable dermatologist you can refer to. My advice is to refer only to dermatologists who do not have a medi-spa, to avoid the possibility of competition for your client.

It is helpful to understand the impact that Retin A, Accutane and HRT (Hormone Replacement Therapy) have on the skin.

If the female client is pregnant or nursing, you need to err on the side of caution. Safety is always first. Check with her doctor if you are in doubt. The reason is not that you will cause any harm to your pregnant client necessarily, however, if anything goes wrong (unrelated to whatever service you have given to her), you do not want your name on the list of possible causes.

INTAKE FORM CONTRAINDICATIONS

The list of possible contraindications is endless, so here are just a few.

Includes but is not limited to...
- Metal implants
- Disease/illness
- Recent deep exfoliation: what, when?
- Recent or pending cosmetic surgeries, or injectables; location and date?
- Recent facial hair removal; when?
- UV exposure from sun or "sunless tanning" from tanning bed
- Lifestyle choices that may affect the skin, such as smoking

Summary:
If you will be using electrical equipment on your clients, then you must be sure to inquire about metal implants.

If they are going through chemo or radiation, you will need to note that and edit your service accordingly.

Recent deep exfoliation such as laser or deep peels must be noted so you can edit your service accordingly.

Cosmetic surgeries or injectables....massage over areas of injection is not advised for a certain amount of time.

Recent facial hair removal and UV exposure are elements that can affect results of a peel.

Lifestyle choices, such as smoking – not that we are to judge whether somebody smokes or not, but sometimes that can affect the skin, so it helpful to know if that may contribute to a client's current skin condition.

NOTE: I want to tell you a story that occurred when I had my spa. A woman came in and asked me about microdermabrasion. Through the process of talking with her, it came out that she had heard somewhere that if you have microdermabrasion followed by using a tanning bed, the result would be a better tan. I turned her away immediately. In no way was I going to participate in providing microdermabrasion as a tanning bed prep. (Sometimes you just have to say NO).

Intake Form – Issues and Goals:
- ○ Top 3 skin care complaints (or goals)
- ○ Previous skin care services; how often?
- ○ Likes and dislikes about previous facials, if any?

Summary:
Issues and goals. There is no right or wrong answer here. The answers are almost always the same. It will most often be about breakouts, wrinkles or "sun spots." This question gets the conversation started and it is usually in this part of the intake process where you receive helpful information as they start talking and you start writing things down.

Previous skin care services. You want to know if they have had any previous skin care services and how often. This can give you an idea regarding whether or not they will become a regular client. If their answer includes a long list of Estheticians they have been unhappy with, it would behoove you to find out why.

Likes and dislikes. This is a great question because the answers you will receive are not only interesting, but it will tell you what to do or not do. Some of the answers I have received are: "The room is too hot, I don't like bright lights in my face. I'm claustrophobic. I don't like to be covered up." Note all of these details in their file and next time they come in, you can customize their experience to avoid these issues…which is a great step toward securing a loyal, repeat client.

INTAKE FORM – HOME CARE

Right here is where retail sales/home care products begin. It is crucial to find out what, if any, home care protocols and products they are currently using.

- Over-the-counter, department store, grocery store, MLM, or professional
- Frequency of cleansing per day
- Tools used: Hands, loofah, washcloth, sponge, cotton pads
- Toner
- Moisturizer
- Exfoliant
- Serums
- Eye cream
- Sun protection
- Other

Summary:
During this section of the intake process, your new client will provide answers to your questions that give you an opportunity to show off your skin care knowledge. For example, if the client tells you he or she is using a loofa on the face, and you see broken capillaries there, you have a great opportunity to explain all the reasons that using a loofa on the face is a bad idea.

What I have found with many people who believe they have naturally problematic skin is that their skin is not actually the culprit. When you get to this part of the Intake Form, you may discover that the problem is specifically what they are doing to their skin. In other words, they are causing the skin issues themselves.

Perhaps you will note that the client is using the wrong moisturizer. For example, they may be using a moisturizer that is a low-quality product, or it may be too rich and heavy for their skin which may be causing breakouts or overproduction of oil. When you explain this to them, they will totally tune into what you are saying, and they will listen carefully. This point in the intake process is where the introduction to home care products and retail sales begins.

Lots of people do not exfoliate. In fact, they do not even know what the word "exfoliate" means. This gives you the opportunity to explain the importance of exfoliation and the differences between the various exfoliation options, such as manual exfoliation and AHAs.

If they are not using serums, or if they are using a serum from some weird celebrity branded product line that has convinced them serums are one-size-fits all, you can explain how serums work, how they differ, and what they are supposed to do.

Many people are not wearing eye creams and oftentimes they should be. You can explain how eye cream works, how thin the skin is in that area, and how to apply eye cream.

As for sun protection, Estheticians know the difference between sun block and chemical sunscreen. Many people do not realize that some states have or will soon be banning products which contain certain problematic ingredients. This is a great time to do your research and bring in the wonderful new sunscreens that meet the new requirements.

Even if your state does not ban the problematic sunscreen ingredients, your clients will likely be going on vacation, and if they happen to be headed to the Hawaiian Islands, those problematic ingredients have already been banned there. So this is a perfect opportunity to become the go-to provider of Hawaii-friendly sunscreens.

The little bits of information that you can provide to clients at this early stage in your relationship with them will increase their comfort level and trust in you, which will positively impact the successful future of your esthetics practice.

Q&A: "Do you Exfoliate?"

This is my favorite question on the Intake Form because there is almost always an opportunity to show off esthetics brilliance!

These are the most common answers I receive when I ask: "Do you exfoliate?"

- No
- Yes. St. Ives Apricot Scrub
- Yes. Department store product
- Yes. Retin A

Any of these answers will give you the perfect opportunity to explain exfoliation. That is the most common conversation I have with a new client.

My favorite answer is when they say no, they do not exfoliate because after I have exfoliated them during the facial and then apply a serum, they walk out thinking I am literally an Esthetician rock star. (Which I am, of course!)

Notes & Records

It is the Esthetician's job to provide guidance that will extend the benefits of the facial. Therefore, it is imperative to keep really good notes and refer to them often so you can guide your clients.

The last page of your self-made Intake Form should be a page with blank lines to be used for filling in the date and writing down pertinent information about that day's facial service. You might want to note everything you used that day such as products, exfoliation technique, serums, mask, and equipment. The next time the client comes in, review those notes before her facial so you can change a few components. That is how easy it is to customize facials and not give your clients the exact same service every time they come in.

Additionally, you can refresh your memory as to any particular condition she may have been struggling with at her last appointment so you can determine whether there has been any improvement. Based upon that information, you can then calculate what her next service should be.

You also would add to this section which products she purchased so that next time she comes in you can ask her, "How are those products working for you? What do you like? Do you have any questions?"

And be sure to note any upcoming travel plans she may have so you will recognize the possible cause of any dehydration or hyperpigmentation that might result. And don't hesitate to record personal details about her family or her work so you can inquire about that next time. This shows an expression of interest in your client, and it will go a long way to further the client bond.

FORMULA STEP 5: Home Care

There are no two ways about it: **Retail matters**. That's because retail sales are maximum profit with minimal effort.

It is very easy to assess profitability when you compare facial services to retail sales: Facial treatments require time and overhead, such as an Esthetician who must be compensated, costs of back bar product, supplies, laundry, and furniture. On the other hand, retail sales require nothing but a little shelf space.

Once clients are hooked on the importance of home care products, he or she can replenish their supply repeatedly without the involvement of an Esthetician. A $200 purchase of skin care products can happen in 10 minutes or less via the receptionist, an email, a phone call, or a private/client-only password-protected e-store. Without overhead costs, retail sales are pure profit.

While there are many paths an Esthetician can take to find financial success, retail sales will always be a vital component.

PRIORITIES

Home Care Retail

I am quite certain that few (if any?) Estheticians working today got into this business with the goal of becoming a salesperson. Yet sales of home care products are a fundamental element of an Esthetician's work..

It is part an Esthetician's job to take care of the client's skin, not just give her a facial. Estheticians are trained to know how to extend the life of the facial so that their client's skin is glowing all the time.

When a client has a facial, the benefits last a few days, and what happens after that depends entirely upon what the client is doing at home. I always say: What the Esthetician can do is 50% of a client's good skin health, and the other 50% depends upon what the client does at home.

Therefore, the formula for great skin is a joint effort between the Esthetician and the client, and here are the two most important elements:

1. Regular facials, the specifics of which are determined by the Esthetician based upon his or her knowledge and training as it applies to the client's current needs.
2. Home care designed by the Esthetician geared toward extending the benefits of the facial by utilizing high-quality professional skin care products and written protocols.

This means, for a client to receive and maintain maximum benefit, the Esthetician must guide her client's skin care routine. Otherwise, if the client is assessing the overall condition of her skin based solely upon the facial, that client is going to think "Yeah, it was a nice facial, and my skin looks pretty good right now. But I don't see any long-term improvement in my skin, so I will just go someplace for a facial once in a while on special occasions."

Whereas if the client is having regular facials <u>and</u> using home care products and protocols which are provided by her Esthetician, then that client not only looks and feels amazing long after the facial is over, but her skin continues to improve with – and in between -- each subsequent facial. And who deserves the credit for that? The Esthetician, of course.

Make it Easy. Make home care easy for your clients. Start slowly and work up to their budget, if necessary. Add additional products as they get used to (and fall in love with) having great skin. For example, perhaps their first skin care protocol does not include a sunscreen, but maybe in the summer they will want to add one.

Make it easy for them to replenish their products when needed. Adjust their product regimen as the skin's needs change, or as the seasons change, or as their hormones change. It goes without saying (but I will say it anyway), if a Professional Esthetician has a client on the same serum for an entire decade, that Esthetician is not doing his or her job, or is not properly educated.

RETAIL SALES ORGANICALLY

If an Esthetician is properly trained, retail sales will happen organically, with no "hard sell" tactics needed. It is up to the Esthetician to figure out which retail sales approach best fits him or her.

For me, the foundation for the client's purchase of home care retail products happens during the facial. It might begin during the Intake Process as I discuss the products the client is currently using at home, and it will most assuredly continue as I explain to the new client the products I have chosen to use during the facial.

By the time the facial is over, without fail, the new client is asking me for my recommendations regarding home care products. With very little effort, a retail sale is made, and a loyal client is born. It really is that easy.

AN ESTHETICIAN'S DUTY

It is the Esthetician's <u>duty</u> to provide home care education and recommendations for their clients, including written "how-to" instructions. It is our job to educate clients about the benefits of our retail products. It is also our duty to explain clearly that proper home care extends the benefits of the facial treatment which will result in continued good skin health.

Another of the Esthetician's jobs is to make sure clients are comfortable with the ingredients and sufficiently understand the benefits of each product. To assure repeat retail sales, it is vital that clients feel confident the products will be a worthwhile investment for them. And for that to happen, the Esthetician must believe it!

Retail profits will surely suffer if the Esthetician does not believe in the products he or she is selling, and that is another reason manufacturers' Product Knowledge classes are essential to every Professional Esthetician. Even if the Esthetician manages to convince a client to purchase products once, there is no guarantee they will buy them a second time. In fact, if a client feels pressure to purchase products, they will likely never return to that Esthetician. There is a "psychology of esthetics," and this is a perfect example of that.

It is also the Esthetician's responsibility to keep records of client purchases for future reference. That way, the client can easily replenish his or her home care products with or without assistance from the Esthetician. As I mentioned earlier, I regularly get requests from long-term clients asking for things like "the stuff in the silver bottle" or "my morning face wash" or "my spritzer." I know that means "serum," "cleanser" and "toner," but I must rely on the client's file to see which specific product she is currently using. This is an example of providing great customer service.

INTRODUCTION TO HOME CARE

The first appointment is different. The first appointment is longer, of course, because there is more to do. There is a consultation and a detailed intake process wherein the Esthetician will gather pertinent information from the client.

There is also information the Esthetician must impart to the client during the first appointment. And there may be questions from the client that the Esthetician may have to answer as this fledgling relationship begins. That is why the first appointment is lengthy and must be scheduled accordingly so that you will have ample time to complete these important steps.

Here is how I do it:

Explain the process. I prefer to do the talking during the first approximately 1/3 of the facial. I will even explain that to the client by saying something like: "Because this is your first appointment with me, I am going to talk you through everything that I am going to do so you can become familiar with my equipment and my tools, as well as any noises you might hear. But I promise I won't put you through this process during subsequent facials." (I make a little joke out of it by saying something like, "Then I'll shut up and let you relax," and they chuckle.)

It is important to warn the new client of any upcoming experience that may jar them a bit, such as, "Now I am going to put my mag lamp over your face, and I'm going to touch your face….. I'm going to put eye pads on you, and this is what I am looking for."

You can also go further and inform them, "I've decided I'm going to use (this form of) exfoliation and it's going to have steam with it, and I'm going to use my Skin Spatula." Whatever it is, tell them about it during this first appointment. You do not have to provide too much detail, just enough to circumvent any surprises or discomfort.

When you are about to put something cool on them, or you will be using a piece of equipment that will make noise, you want to say: "You are going to feel something cool on your face" or "you will hear a buzzing sound, sort of like a bee…that is my high frequency machine."

Products. Lastly, be sure to explain all products that are being used and tell them why. This really furthers their interest in home care. As an example, you might say, "I am going to use this serum on you today because winter is here and you're probably going to get a bit dry, so I am going to prep your skin with Hyaluronic Serum." You can take this a step further and explain Hyaluronic Serum, and why your professional products are of a higher quality than what they will find online.

These bits of info are more important than you might think because this leads directly to effortless home care retail sales. 95% of the time, when I have completed a client's first facial, they will ask to buy the products that I used in their facial, or whatever else I recommend. (And I am not exaggerating that percentage!)

Successful retail sales are all about how well you have laid the foundation. This is how you build trust. They will trust your products, and they will rely on your guidance.

Ask yourself these questions:

- Does this client understand how important home care products are?
- Does this client understand why my guidance regarding home care products is essential?
- Does this client understand that I will be changing things as needed (and why)?
- Does this client know that I will be checking in with them regularly?

This extra bit of effort on the Esthetician's part will bring the client to a higher level of trust and comfort, which means she is not going to be looking for products online, nor will she seek out other Estheticians. She is going to stay with you and she going to trust you.

BEHIND THE SCENES: A Note to Spa Owners

One of the biggest financial mistakes I see spa owners make is not allowing extra time before and after a new client's first appointment. Instead, they have their Estheticians running from client to client with barely enough time to change the sheets on the facial bed. This is an enormous error.

While the typical massage department must rely on services for income, the opposite is true in the esthetics department because of the endless opportunities for retail sales. Once the connection between an Esthetician and her client has been established, the client will replenish her home care products on an ongoing basis -- with or without a facial service. So, while there is a cap on the amount of profit a service can provide, the profit from retail sales is unlimited.

Another reason to factor in extra time between clients is that new clients may have never been face-to-face with an Esthetician. These clients may have questions about the facial and their skin condition, as well as curiosity about the products and equipment that were used during the facial. And they almost always want advice about home care. It is an important part of the Esthetician's job to answer the client's questions and make the client feel comfortable. That is how clients bond with their Estheticians, and that is how loyal clients are created.

HOW TO GUARANTEE CLIENTS BUY PRODUCTS ONLY FROM YOU:
20% off to those who have monthly facials!

Yes, it's possible. I know this sounds like a big number, but hear me out. Here is how to guarantee clients will buy products only from you rather than online sources:

Hopefully you have educated your clients about product diversion, and you have explained that you are a Solo Esthetician or the owner of a small esthetics business, and therefore you purchase in small batches which means your products are always fresh, stored well, etc.

From there, you would create a VIP program wherein clients would commit to having a regular facial with you monthly or every six weeks (whatever your number is). Those clients who commit to regular facials are entitled to purchase their retail home care products at 20% off.

I know 20% off sounds like a big number but let me do the math for you. First, it has to be a big number. It cannot be 10% or 15% or no one will pay attention because they will probably get a better deal on Amazon. So, you've got to have a hefty number, and I think 20% is that number.

Here is the financial benefit:

- You will have a lot more people coming in for facials because in order to take advantage of the 20% off, they are going to have to <u>commit</u> to regularly scheduled facials. This will bring a lot of additional income from facials. So right there, your profit has increased exponentially.

But there's more!

- All of those clients who are bringing you additional service income will now also be purchasing products from you regularly. So you will enjoy all of that additional retail income!

The 20% discount can be offset by adding a tiny amount – 25 cents, for example – to the retail price of your products. (You can charge whatever you want for your products, but obviously don't go crazy.)

This is a lot of additional income for you, and it is great for the clients because they are getting fresh, properly stored, high-quality products that have been selected by the Esthetician specifically for each client, at that particular time, for their specific skin condition. Additionally, clients will be having regular facials and using proper home care products, which of course means their skin is always going to look fabulous. And that is a wonderful reflection on you!

BEHIND THE SCENES: A Note to Spa Owners

It is in your best interest to provide educational opportunities to your Estheticians. Skin analysis and product knowledge classes are key. Keep retail sales in-house. If your clientele is transient such as in a resort spa, look to hire personable Estheticians who really like people, as oftentimes the priority of these clients is simply a pleasant experience.

Give your Estheticians incentives such as commission paid on retail sales, and vouchers or discounts on products to encourage them to use the products on themselves at home so they are intimately familiar with each product. To avoid employees using their discount to purchase unlimited products for friends, give vouchers instead.

Example of a voucher: If employees are allowed a percentage discount, there is no way to police whether they are buying products for their own use or are extending the discount to others. However, if you reward them with a $50 voucher (or whatever amount you choose), which is only awarded when they reach a pre-determined retail sales goal, they are likely to spend it on themselves. But even if they use it on a friend, you still are only out $50 which is much better than a discount on unlimited products.

My goal is to build a life that I don't need a vacation from.
~Rob Hill, Sr.

6 MARKETING

THE FIRST IMPRESSION

You have heard the saying, "You don't get a second chance to make a first impression." Well, in most cases, it's true. Therefore, this is something we must consider when growing a successful esthetics business.

A Connection

The first contact potential clients have with your esthetics business might be online. Social media has changed the communication landscape, that's for sure. Gone are the days when clients and potential clients received personal service on the phone when scheduling their appointments. It really is a great loss because this personal form of contact was the best chance for the business to make a great first impression and set themselves apart. It was also an opportunity to upsell their services even before an appointment was made.

Also gone are personal phone calls to remind clients of their upcoming appointments. These days, it is online appointment scheduling and reminders (if any) by email or text. Yes, it is extremely convenient for us, but it is a mistake for today's Estheticians to completely neglect personal interaction in their business-building strategy.

When it comes to success in the spa business, people buy from people with whom they feel a connection. In other words, human beings do not begin to really **care** until we personally connect. We want to know: "Do you understand ME?"

Unfortunately, most of us are doing it backwards because we have been taught to approach new clients with non-priority tactics rather than our first priority being to create a connection. We are missing the most important aspect of our potential success which is that people don't care about the name of the person or the name of the business until they care about the person…in other words, until they feel a connection.

SOCIAL MEDIA MARKETING

Has social media lost its power of persuasion?

For some of us, it seems like only yesterday that social media marketing was a new and exciting opportunity. (And it was!) But times have changed and these days, social media is commonplace, so you better know how to get the most out of it. Ask yourself why you are online and then use the answer to determine your goals and specifically how social media can help you meet those goals.

Before embarking on a social media campaign, it is important to have a clearly defined goal and to identify an intended outcome. For example, have you done a detailed audience analysis? Is your goal to entice people to sign up for your mailing list? Do you want to sell them a particular product or service? What is your specific goal?

The Road to Mediocrity. Duplicating what everyone else is doing is the fastest way to mediocrity, and there is no way to stand out when you are mediocre. You blend in with all the others which makes you unremarkable and forgettable. By limiting yourself only to social media marketing, you run the risk of ignoring potential clients such as anti-aging clients -- and more specifically, the Baby Boomer generation -- some of which may be using social media, but not necessarily to research products and services.

Consumers are hit with a constant barrage of information from television, social media, emails, etc. Our email address is required for practically everything, and our personal info ends up in a multitude of databases used for marketing purposes.

Yet, I often hear spa consultants advise Estheticians to "capture" people's email addresses to be used for marketing purposes. That is stale and inefficient advice because we, as a society, are drowning in emails, so this type of covert "capture email" marketing is no longer effective.

I am not suggesting these sorts of marketing strategies will not work for somebody, but it is not necessarily the best choice for Estheticians. Cheaper and faster does not mean more effective. Use your social media strategies as one tool in your marketing kit, but not at the expense of abandoning personal contact with clients and potential clients.

E-Newsletters. Far too often, e-newsletters are not being read and/or are being unsubscribed from. Even if the e-newsletters are being opened, they are usually not eliciting a response from clients or potential clients. Emails are being ignored or deleted because not only is it impossible to stand out in somebody's email box with limited visible info (such as the sender's name and subject line), but email marketing has become an annoyance.

Even more annoying, I think, is the practice of sending unsolicited text messages to promote goods and services. Not only is this an interruption to a client's day, but depending upon a person's text message plan, they could be charged for those texts. In our business, a source of annoyance is definitely <u>not</u> what we want to be.

Business owners need to know where to draw the line
on social media marketing.

Direct Mail. Let's take a look at direct mail, also known as snail mail or hard copy, which believe it or not, has an advantage over email and e-newsletters. Most importantly, the recipient will at least have the hard copy in their hand, even if it is just briefly, long enough to carry it to the recycle bin. The opposite is true with email or e-newsletters as those are too easy to just skip right over and not bother to open.

If you are going to try direct mail, be sure to keep it simple. Have the most important info at the top, and believe it or not, the most important info is not your logo, name, or contact info. If you waste that important top spot by starting with your company name or logo or some cutesy introduction, you've lost them. They will not bother to read further, and therefore will miss your message entirely. However, if you capture their attention with essential information at the top of the page, they will keep reading down the page and will seek out your company info at the bottom.

Include a photo. For whatever reason, research shows that people will look carefully at something that contains a photo of people. Maybe it is just simple curiosity, but it will get their attention. And once you have snagged their interest, they will scan the rest of the page to figure out who these people are and what they have to offer.

Make an impression with the envelope. Make it personal by hand-addressing the envelope so it will not look like all the other solicitations that come in the mail. Stand out by using an interesting envelope such as one with color, pattern or design.

Make it easy to read. Choose an easy-on-the-eyes color and print, such as a dark-colored text on a light-colored background with simple font. Do not force clients and potential clients to work hard to read your message... or they won't. For example, if the font is so small that they will have to get up and fetch their reading glasses, they'll likely skip it...and you.

Postcards. Maybe. However, postcards are very common which means they do not stand out. Postcards may be cheaper but remember, cheaper does not mean better or more effective. If you give postcards a try, be sure to measure the response by including a "Call to Action" so you will know how many recipients responded.

DEMOGRAPHICS

Selling Treatments....or Creating Loyal Clients?

Have you ever heard the term "cast a wide net and hope you catch something"? That is exactly what many Estheticians are doing as they try to market themselves. They are spending too much money trying random marketing tactics, without knowing if those strategies are working.

A better strategy is what I call "measurable marketing," which is the opposite of casting a wide net and hoping you catch something. In other words, if you cannot track a marketing strategy's success, then don't use it.

For example, offering discounted services may bring bodies in your door, but once the discounted price is gone, so will those clients be. Instead, choose marketing strategies that will serve the goal of creating long-term loyal clients; clients who will make and keep regular appointments and will purchase retail products from you. Treat them well, for at any moment, you are only one mistake away from losing them to another Esthetician.

DEFINING YOUR TARGET MARKET

Before choosing a marketing strategy, you must research and carefully consider your preferred demographic. Determine where your desired clientele gets their information, and do not be afraid to think outside the box a little.

Know your Brand. Marketing your business without first defining your brand, your image, and your target market rarely works, and in fact is a big mistake and a monumental waste of money. Before embarking on a marketing campaign, you must determine who you want to be.

How do you want to be identified? Do you want to be trendy, feminine, masculine, coed, clinical, tranquil, cosmopolitan, European, metrosexual, millennial? Once that's been decided, then your marketing strategies should always further your brand.

Know your Customers. Before planning a service menu or selecting a product line, you must consider whether your clients will be predominantly women, men, college students, Baby Boomers, etc. You should also contemplate the income level, ethnicity(s), and possible time constraints when setting your menu. Income level obviously relates to pricing; ethnicity dictates what types of treatments will do well on your menu, and it is imperative that you consider the needs of working women and men and stay-at-home moms and dads regarding hours and days of operation.

Once you have determined your demographic, you can then more capably decide whether to offer spa treatments, clinical treatments, or both, as well as what level of products to use and sell. Also consider elements such as your desired demographic's income level or time constraints. How about the needs of working moms who would be interested in evening appointments? Or soccer moms who are tied up most weekends during soccer season.

Maybe you will have clients who require specific products, such as ethnic skin and teen skin. It is wise to let your service menu and product lines be dictated by your demographic. Maybe waxing or sugaring will be your big thing. Maybe it will be men's services. These things have to be figured out before you start spending money on marketing.

Where does your demographic get their info? Once you have determined who your clients are (or who you want them to be), then you must figure out where your desired demographic gets their information. Be creative. To stand out and get noticed, you must be creative.

Does your desired demographic read a local city-wide newspaper, or a smaller neighborhood newspaper? Where I live, there is a neighborhood newspaper that comes in the mail, and I prefer that one over the regular city-wide newspaper because the smaller one is specific to my area. For advertising purposes, the smaller newspaper is typically a much less expensive option, and it will target potential clients who are in your immediate area.

Perhaps your demographic listens to the radio on the way to work? Now that's an interesting concept, and I will tell you a little story about why you must be careful with that. Years ago, I served on a panel at one of our trade shows where a member of the audience asked the question about the best way to advertise. One of my fellow panelists responded that the radio was a really good way to do it and then went into detail about the perks of radio advertising.

I did not want to correct my counterpart but in my mind, I just wanted to scream "NO!" Radio may be a good investment if it fits your demographic but for the rest of us, it is way too expensive. Not only that, but clients do not necessarily listen to the radio. The moral to that story is that radio advertising does not work for everyone which is why you must not believe everything you hear (even if it's from a speaker at a trade show).

Maybe your desired demographic gets their information at church. Or perhaps your desired clientele is made up of college students and in that case, you can check to see if there is a sorority/fraternity blog or podcast that accepts outside advertising.

If you own a young, trendy waxing studio, social media might be great for you but do not overlook other possible resources such as college publications and local gyms.

If your business is in upscale suburbia, think about country clubs, golf courses, yoga and Pilates studios; and anywhere mommies might hang out such as gymnastics and karate studios.

YOUR PREFERRED DEMOGRAPHIC

The benefit of identifying your demographic before choosing marketing strategies is that then you are able to focus on specific strategies that will lead directly to your long-term goals – which of course is all about creating loyal clients and enjoying financial freedom.

Below are some of the most common demographics, and a few points to consider when contemplating your desired demographic. I want to stress, however, that this is a generalization based upon past research, but times are always changing and so will this data.

"BABY BOOMER": Those born during a demographic birth boom of 1946-1964, following World War II.

Do not make the mistake of underestimating this lucrative demographic. They are typically great clients for many reasons: They are very interested in anti-aging products and services. They typically do not have children at home and are often retired which gives them more time and more money to spend on regular esthetics services and home care products.

On the other hand, they may have special considerations such as perhaps their eyesight might be giving them a little trouble. In that case, you may want to use bigger fonts on your menu and marketing materials (as I have done with this book).

Also helpful is using contrasting colors, such as black print on a light paper and vice versa. You might want to have brighter light in your retail area as well as a magnifying glass within easy reach to make it easier for the client to read the product labels.

In many cases, however, this demographic may not be actively involved with social media, and there is a pretty good chance that some of them may not care for online scheduling. This means, if you are only utilizing social media and online services to connect, you could be missing out on an extremely profitable group of potential clients.

WOMEN: Generally enjoy the shopping experience.

Typically this demographic makes up the majority of most Estheticians' client base, so we have a lot of experience with this group. The study of women and how they shop is really quite fascinating, I think. Generally speaking, most women like most things about shopping.

Interestingly, when a woman comes in for a facial, she prefers to do any retail shopping on her way in, rather than on her way out. For example, when a women has just finished having a facial, she may feel a bit disheveled, maybe her hair is messy, her makeup has been removed and she may be in a deep post-facial fog, so things may not be registering clearly. For those reasons, it is important to encourage her to shop on her way in. This is yet another reason to plan extra time between facials, to give the client some time when she arrives to look around, notice what you are selling, note what is displayed on your counter, check out your retail area, etc.

Women do like to read the front of the package before purchasing. This is really important so you want to make sure they can read the front of the package, because if they can't read it, they will put it down and they won't buy it.

Women will spend more time and money when they are shopping with a friend. This is another reason extra time is a good idea. So if two female friends are coming in for facials at the same time, be sure they have sufficient time together to do some shopping in your retail area.

Studies show one thing women do not like about shopping is having to bend down to the bottom shelf to reach something. (The exception is younger women.)

And lastly, mirrors inside treatment rooms. This is a mistake that Estheticians may not realize they are making. If you put a mirror inside your treatment room, it is going to slow down the departure of your female clients. So, while having a mirror accessible is a good idea, it is better to have it somewhere other than inside your treatment room.

MEN: Generally do not enjoy the shopping experience.

The climate is rapidly changing when it comes to male shoppers because men of today are becoming more interested in spa, facial and skin care products than in previous generations. Personally, I have always loved my male clients. I found my male clients to be wonderfully uncomplicated. By that I mean that they listened to what I was recommending, they followed my suggestions, and they used the products properly.

However, research still shows that the majority of men who are shopping in a spa or esthetics business are doing so with their female significant others in mind. This demographic does not typically enjoy the browsing/shopping process (at least when it comes to skin care) as much as women do. This doesn't mean men aren't interested in skin care or products. It simply means they don't necessarily like shopping for it.

It is a good practice for those Estheticians who have -- or want -- a male clientele -- to have men's purchases ready to go so they can get in and get out quickly. Male shoppers typically like written info, so have literature easily accessible on the retail shelf. In other words, do not force them to ask for the literature or information. It is also a good idea to keep gentlemen's preferences in mind when choosing displays, packaging, testers etc.

YOUTH: In my opinion, this is an enormous untapped market for both male and female youth. And by "youth" I am referring to high school/college age, although the advice here could technically apply for any age. I developed a lucrative business based upon the children of my clients as they grew up and moved on to high school and college.

A common issue for this age group is acne which is often a result of fluctuating hormones. Of course, Estheticians cannot balance the hormones, but we can address the acne topically. However, if the acne is of a higher grade, we must refer out to a dermatologist or hormone specialist.

When environmental aspects are the culprit, however, there is much Estheticians can do to help. For example, I have seen acne mechanica appear on the forehead due to the wearing of baseball caps. This can be a simple fix utilizing the Esthetician's knowledge to teach proper skin care and provide high-quality products and written protocols. That is exactly what I did, and it worked very well for me.

The College Dorm Kit. When this age group left for college, they took with them a selection of products and written instructions curated by me to address their specific skin care concerns. I called it "The College Dorm Skin Care Kit."

I made it extremely easy for the college students to replenish their skin care products. To do that, I kept mom or dad's credit card on file and with their permission, I would replenish their college-aged children's skin care products as needed. The college student could simply send me an email and I would pack up their products, charge the parent's credit card, and ship the package directly to the student.

Because they were getting their products from me, Mom or Dad knew their children were always using the best products that had been chosen specifically to fit the needs of their child.

Educate. Another service we can offer to this age group is education. (A lot of education!) One of the ways I offered education was to go to middle school and/or high school students directly.

With the school's permission, you can do this after school or at lunchtime on the school grounds. Or invite a Boy Scout or Girl Scout troop, sports team, or class to your place of business. Another idea is to donate a group consultation to a school auction in your area.

I visited a couple of schools and I brought my skin scanner with me. Everybody gathered in one of the vacant classrooms after school had ended for the day. The audience was made up of 8th graders and their moms. (Dads were invited but only moms showed up.)

I gave a short presentation and then I invited a few volunteers to try my skin scanner. What I didn't realize the first time I did this was how much interest there would be in my skin scanner. It was a miscalculation on my part, for sure! It was this experience that taught me the power of the skin scanner. It has such a strong visual impact, and it immediately piques the viewer's interest regarding proper skin care. I had samples and literature with me, and I ended up with several new clients (mostly the moms, which was perfectly fine with me!).

As popular as the skin scanner was, the problem for me was that the skin scanner portion of my presentation took much more time than I had expected, so it cut into the time I had planned for skin care education. That said, I would still recommend this marketing strategy, but I would advise adjusting the time allotted for the presentation.

SENIORS: The over-70 crowd.

This is a really great opportunity for specialty treatments and home care products for very mature skin.

Keep in mind not everybody in the over 70 demographic wants to get plastic surgery or fillers. Some of them just want to take really good care of their skin. This is a great niche for Estheticians to fill. This demographic is typically interested in easy-to-follow home care protocols and high-quality products.

As with any demographic, you must first figure out where they get their information. It could be where everybody else gets their info, but it also could be specific to where they are in their life. They could be in a senior care facility, or they could get their information from church. Perhaps these are the parents or grandparents of your existing clients, so you could simply add a "senior section" in your newsletter.

Depending upon the age and the situation, transportation may be an obstacle for some seniors should they wish to come to your business for a facial service. If you want to cultivate this demographic, you may want to figure out a way to solve the transportation problem. For example, you can research transportation options for seniors and provide that information to them.

And as with restaurants, theaters, etc., senior discounts are always appreciated.

SOCIAL MEDIA: HOW MUCH IS TOO MUCH?

"Likes" and "Follows" do not translate to new business for Estheticians. They translate to new business for the social media site and its advertisers.

If social media marketing is working for you, which means it is driving people to your website and to your esthetics business, then that is fabulous. Keep doing it. Social media is definitely a handy way to notify clients of last-minute openings and upcoming events.

However, if you are using social media to market your business, you must be certain that you are tracking the outcome. And if those numbers are not meeting your goals, that's your cue not to rely solely on social media. Perhaps it's time to back off that marketing strategy.

THE DOWNSIDE OF SOCIAL MEDIA FOR BUSINESS

Time consuming. Although social media can be fun, when it comes to marketing your business, it is not typically the best use of time because the required monitoring of your pages – if done properly --

can be overly time-consuming. An Esthetician makes a lot more money working in the treatment room than he or she does by spending time on social media. So if social media efforts are not bringing in clients and increasing your income, then it is likely wasting a lot of your income-producing time.

It is boring. Another thing to consider is that everybody is marketing on social media all the time which means you will likely blend in with everyone else. You won't stand out. You are just one of millions who are doing it this way. If it is not regularly bringing you new clients and financial reward, don't fall into the trap of doing something just because everyone else is doing it.

Politically Correct. Depending upon how well you are able to control yourself as far as opinions about things that are not related to your business (politics, religion, etc.), sometimes you can unknowingly push people away rather than bringing them in. If you get too personal, or you get mad at somebody, or you "like" something others might consider questionable, you can tarnish your professional reputation. When it comes to social media, you might think you can keep your personal and business lives separate, but they inevitably bleed into each other.

Be sure that you have a plan for exactly how you will use social media to market yourself and your business and keep your personal and professional selves as separate as possible.

In Summary. While it is easy to follow the crowd into the land of social media, that is not necessarily the best path to financial success in the esthetics business. We must very carefully consider the totality of our marketing strategies. Social media has its place, but in our business specifically, we must not forget the need for personal contact outside of the treatment room.

ONLINE SCHEDULING

Online scheduling is a great thing for sure, and it definitely should be one of the tools in your tool kit because most people are internet

THE HEART OF ESTHETICS

savvy these days. The convenience to both the client and the Esthetician is noteworthy. Clients can make an appointment anytime, such as outside of regular business hours, in the middle of the night wearing their pajamas. And an enormous advantage for the Esthetician or spa is that they do not have to pay anyone to answer the phone and deal with appointment scheduling.

On the other hand, there are some major drawbacks to relying only on online scheduling. Firstly, there is no live person to which a potential new client can ask questions or who can explain the various facial options. And let's not forget that even in this age of the internet, there still are some people who may be intimidated or annoyed by the online process. (Most likely, those of us who grew up in the age of personal service, which has since been replaced by online everything.)

But the greatest loss is the very important first conversation wherein a potential new client can ask questions and have guidance as they attempt to navigate the service menu. These are important **moments of truth** that can make or break an esthetics business or spa.

Another drawback is that online scheduling leaves new clients having to decide which facial they should have, which I wholeheartedly believe is the Esthetician's job. In my opinion, That is **not** the job of the client or potential client. Estheticians are the ones who have the training therefore we must participate in the decision regarding which service a client needs.

That said, if you want to limit your client base only to online savvy customers, that's okay. But by doing that, you could be missing a whole group of people who do not necessarily like online scheduling, especially for the first appointment when they may have a lot of questions.

We are in an intimate business in which success is measured by our personal connection with people.

MARKETING IDEAS

If you build it, will anyone come?

On the topic of marketing efforts, there is a very important aspect that is too often overlooked. And here it is: When you spend your hard-earned money on any sort of marketing strategy, you should have some way to measure its success.

Ban the Clutter. An effective marketer knows that for his or her message to stand out, it must be very clear and to the point. There is a lot of information competing for the customer's attention, so your message should be void of all unnecessary blah-blah-blah that a prospective customer does not need to read, hear or view.

In other words, any marketing message – if it's going to produce results – needs to cut through the clutter. If the message is unclear, too complex, or too long, it won't cut through and the result will be that the marketer has failed to engage the customer. The message has fallen on deaf ears.

MARKETING STRATEGIES

In this section, we are going to go into very specific strategies with which to effectively market your esthetics business. Most of these ideas will cost you nothing, except a little time and a bit of effort. We will start with relatively traditional strategies and then we will move into-out-of-the-box strategies with a goal to create a clientele that reaches beyond what you may have previously considered.

Measurable Marketing. "Measurable" marketing refers to strategies that can be measured in such a way that you are able to assess its effectiveness. To put it another way: If you are not able to measure it, don't do it – especially if it will cost money.

"Measure" in this scenario means that you must be able to calculate the response. For example, how many people took action? How many scheduled an appointment? How many attended the event you were advertising? And most importantly, how many purchased something?

As you know from an earlier chapter of this book, what the prospective client or current client wants to know is "What's in it for me?" Provide the answer to that implied question right from the get-go, and then offer something that will make the prospective client take action.

The First 10 Callers. One of my measurable marketing strategies I nicknamed "The First 10 Callers." For this special, I offered an upgrade as the impetus to entice the client to take action. Here's how I did it:

This special offer included an upgraded mask with the purchase of a facial service. I named this something fun like "Masked Monday" and I would offer the special every Monday for one month.

I chose Monday because it was typically a slow day of the week. I know a lot of Estheticians offer specials around holidays such as Mother's Day, and that's certainly a good thing to do, but everyone does that. I wanted to do it differently so I would stand out, and also to avoid competition with all the other Estheticians offering specials around Mother's Day. I wanted to bring in clients on a traditionally slow day of the week.

If you want to try something like my Masked Monday special, here is how it would work: You would announce that this special is available to the first 10 callers or texters, or however you want them to communicate with you. From there, you will track how many responses you get. Did you get 10? Did you get 1? Or did you get 25? Based upon how many services were booked and the number of products sold will measure how successful this particular marketing strategy was for you.

Here's the best part: If this strategy is working well and clients are responding, there is no need to limit it to 10. Only you know how many people actually responded, so if you want to keep going and offer it to 15 or 20 callers, you can do that! Nobody else will know. But, please note: This is why you should <u>not</u> invite responses via social media, because if viewers are able to see and count the number of responses, they will know when you hit #10 and they will stop responding. It is much better to keep the tally of responses to yourself.

Be sure to advertise this special in ONE location at a time, such as one newspaper or one social media site. The reason for this is that you want to know which source the responses are coming from. Whichever source provides the most responses, that's the one you should keep using. This is "measurable marketing."

INVITE THEM IN

This is so simple, yet it is so often overlooked, This marketing strategy is literally how I built my spa business.

The least expensive and most direct way of reaching clients is simply to invite them in! Grab a friend, hand him or her a pen and paper and drive around the neighborhoods where you would like to snag yourself some new clients. (Obviously, the nearer to your business, the better.)

As you drive down the various streets, have your co-pilot simply write down addresses. Let's say you are on Main Street, write down the house number of every house on Main Street, then go to the next street and do the same thing.

Dear Neighbor Letter.

Prepare a nice "Dear Neighbor" letter to send to those prospective new clients whose addresses you have obtained. Include in the letter your contact info, hours of operation, product lines used, service menu, business card, etc.

I suggest printing this on specialty paper that you can buy at your local office supply store. If you get decorative envelopes, it will help your message stand out and hopefully save it from death-by-recycle-bin. I urge you to hand-address the envelopes so it appears more personal, which is exactly what you are going for.

If you were to compare the price of the paper and postage to the cost of professionally printing a flyer or postcard, or placing an ad in a newspaper, you will find that this method of marketing is much less expensive and much more personal.

Here is an outline of this very simple letter that you can personalize to fit your own business. It is a short, friendly little piece of information in which you are introducing yourself and extending an invitation.

> Dear Neighbor,
>
> My name is Ethel Esthetician and I am the (owner of / Esthetician at) Skin Perfection, which has just opened in the Happy Valley Shopping Center.
>
> I am writing to introduce myself and to invite you to come in for a complimentary _____ (skin evaluation, brow wax, product sample).
>
> I have been in the business for _____ years, my specialty is _____ (add something personal about yourself. What makes you special? What do you do better than anyone else in your area? Give them a list. For example:)
>
> - Sugaring or waxing services (no double dipping!)
> - Stellar sanitation practices
> - Post-grad education
> - Organic products
> - Ample parking
> - Safe location
> - Evening hours
> - A specialty

- High-tech equipment
- Aromatherapy specialist
- No animal testing
- Massage therapist
- Nail technician
- Body treatments
- Extra-wide facial bed for larger clients
- Less disrobing for body treatments
- Time saver facial treatments
- Customized facials
- VIP program

I am enclosing a copy of my menu for you. I hope you will stop in for your complimentary service. I look forward to meeting you.

Thank you for taking the time to read my letter. I hope to see you soon.

Sincerely,

Ethel Esthetician

Personalize your Invitation. It is a good idea to highlight anything about your business, your location, or your services that will entice the reader to accept your invitation. Perhaps you are a long-time resident of your city, or your neighborhood. Anything that you can think of which makes you stand out or personalizes this letter can make an enormous difference.

Assess your Competition. While you are driving around the neighborhood, be on the lookout for other spas and Estheticians in the area. See if you can spot a void, such as services that none of them are offering (or at least not actively promoting). If you can grab a brochure, do it. If not, at least write down the name of the business and get some info online.

If in your research you find a void that you can fill, therein lies your specialty! It may require that you take a few extra esthetics classes, but so what? Become really good at whatever it is the others are not doing and get the word out that you specialize in this service.

Here are some specialty ideas:

- Organic services and products
- Specialized acne services
- Teens and 'Tweens facial services
- Services for mature skin (60+)
- De-stress/aromatherapy services
- "Happy Hour" Facial (serve non-alcoholic beverages)
- Stand-alone eye service
- Targeted services for hyperpigmented hands or décolleté
- Ayurveda treatments
- Warm Winter services (with heated hand treatment)
- Cool Summer services (facial massage with cool globes)
- Imagery/subliminal facial

As you can see, there are many things you can do to stand out both on your service menu and in your neighborhood. For example, you can change things up seasonally by creating a "warm winter" menu. You do not have to create new facial services for this. All you have to do is edit the names of your existing facials so they will fit your winter theme and bring in essential oils and any products you already have that complement the theme. Scents that are reminiscent of winter and products that target dehydration are good choices. Change the colors of the facial bed covering and perhaps offer a heated hand treatment.

Lei Spa. In the summer, you can create a tropical theme simply by adjusting services to accommodate warmer weather. For example, my former spa was located in an area where it could get into the triple digits during the summer and stay that way for a few months. So, beginning in June and running through August, I changed the name of my spa from "Skin Renewal Center" to "Lei Spa" ("Lei" as in the Hawaiian floral necklace.)

On my computer, I printed up menus using tropical-themed paper with the heading changed to "Lei Spa." We decorated with Hawaiian-themed decorations that I got inexpensively online. My staff wore fake leis, we had fake flowers in our hair, we put a grass skirt around the front desk, and we had Hawaiian music playing.

We changed the names of the facials to tropical sounding names, funny ones usually. We had beach balls in various places throughout the spa, and we had sand dollars and actual sand on the retail shelves. It was fun for the staff and for our clients, and we all looked forward to the tropical transformation every year.

In very hot summers, it can be hard to lure people out of their air-conditioned homes, but word got around about Lei Spa and the result was lots of new clients!

Newsletters. As discussed earlier, it is important to make consistent efforts to provide great customer service. The newsletter is an under-used and under-valued method of reaching out to clients and keeping your name in front of them so you will not be forgotten. It is a wonderful way to impart education and information, and to promote your products and services.

This newsletter is not to be confused with e-newsletters and emails. The impact of e-newsletters has faded. That isn't to say it will not come back as a driving force someday, but as of this writing it is not the best way to reach out to most esthetics clients. That's because these days, we are inundated with e-newsletters to the point that people are no longer opening them or paying attention to them. I have to admit, I don't read e-newsletters anymore.

Hard copy newsletters do not have to be professionally prepared. Estheticians can create them on their computer using basic word processing software. It can be as simple as one page, and it can be sent monthly or quarterly -- as long as it is sent regularly.

The primary goal of your newsletter is to educate. Explain things like skin conditions and esthetics terms, or give tips about makeup or sunscreen use. Perhaps let clients know you have recently attended a professional trade show and share something you learned there.

Always mention a service or product you offer which relates to the topic of your newsletter. In other words, present a skin care issue, and then offer the solution. But do remember, this method of marketing is not about selling. This is about "Hello, it's me! I'm thinking about you!"

The goal of the newsletter is simply to keep yourself on their radar, while at the same time reminding them that you are a Professional Esthetician who keeps up with esthetic training, esthetics trends, the latest and greatest products and services, etc.

Mystery Gift Card. Here is another example of "measurable marketing" because with this promotion you are able to determine the number of people who responded, as well as how many of them purchased something.

This is a fun way to entice people to come into your business. Be sure to indicate a specific timeframe for this promotion so it does not go on indefinitely. It should feel exciting and special to the clients, so send an email that says something like this:

> "This email is worth up to $200! Print out this email (or snap a pic) and stop by the spa on Saturday or Sunday, November 3rd or 4th to exchange your email or photo for a surprise gift card worth $20 to $200 in services or 10% to 20% off of retail products!"

During the noted dates of this promotion, have a basket or jar they can reach into and randomly pull out a card that tells them what their discount will be. This is a really fun way to get people in, surprise them and reward them. Because specific action on their part is required, it is measurable and therefore easy to determine if this is a successful marketing strategy for you.

Partner with a Charity. This is something I did with great success. You can partner with a charity by either donating a portion of sales, or you and your staff can participate in a live event. Perhaps they are sponsoring a run or a walk, and you can put together a team. Besides being a compassionate thing to do, partnering with a charity is wonderful exposure for your business, especially the women in your area.

I have done this with large well-known charities, but I prefer to support local non-profits in my area who really need the help. Some examples might be non-profit groups helping animals, children, homeless, and health causes. It is best to choose something you are personally enthusiastic about, but generally speaking, stay away from political or religious charities unless of course that is the specific demographic you are going for.

Advertise the partnership in your newsletter, on your front door, and on social media. Partnering with a charity is a great thing to do, and it feels really good to help. Hopefully, the charity will allow you to use their logo in your marketing materials so you are helping them, and they are helping you.

Career Specials. This is another promotion which not only does something nice for those who are out in the world working hard for us, but also brings potential new clients into our business.

The careers on my list included nurses, doctors, military, emergency personnel, new moms, animal rescue staff, but it can be anybody you are passionate about. If you have a connection to a specific group, by all means tap into that.

I ran a special for court reporters because that is a connection to my previous career. At the time, I had a massage therapist at my spa, so I offered a massage for court reporters at a discounted price. I took this promotion one step further by holding a contest wherein one court reporter a month would get a free massage.

Because I had a solid connection to court reporters, it was easy for me to market to them. If you have a connection to a particular career by way of your family and friends, treat those people to a discount or a free service. This is a wonderful marketing strategy for Estheticians.

You do not have to limit this promotion to only one career. You could have 12 different careers and promote one per month. For example, January is a discount for nurses, February is doctors, etc. If you decide to run this promotion sporadically, each month or a few times per year, I suggest you select months when you are not normally busy because this is a great way to bring people in during the slower months.

Say it with Flowers. I know that Estheticians are typically pretty good about sending birthday cards to their clients, but if you think about it, most of us receive impersonal birthday cards from a variety of businesses all the time. However, Estheticians are different and our business is different. Our business is built on the personal relationships we have with our clients, so we can do better than a birthday card.

Take some time to go through your records and check the annual spend of your clients. If you see someone who has spent quite a lot of money with you, how about doing something out of the ordinary like sending flowers? It will have a far bigger impact than would simply giving a discount on services.

Or how about flowers for an existing client when they have referred a new client to you? I am not suggesting you send an expensive bouquet of flowers. I am referring to something simple like from your garden.

You might take a look at your local floral supply for things like vases, ribbons and flowers. In California, if we have a resale license (which we must have in order to purchase wholesale skin care products and resell them), we can obtain a wholesale account at our local floral supply. I have accounts at a few of them and when you are paying wholesale prices, it is very affordable.

If you deliver the flowers yourself, or have a friend deliver them to a client's place of business, can you imagine the reaction the recipient will have? (Not to mention everyone around her!) Everybody will want to know who the flowers are from…and of course the answer is: Her wonderful Esthetician!

The Wish List. This is something I came up with to solve a problem we were having at my spa which happened around all the major celebrations that involved women, such as birthdays, Valentine's Day, Mother's Day, and Christmas.

The significant others, the husbands, the wives, the boyfriends, the girlfriends of my clients would call the spa wanting to get a gift or a gift certificate for their loved one, and we would always scramble to figure out what we should recommend. After a couple of years, I realized that the solution to this problem was to keep a list of what each regular client preferred as far as services, products, candle scents, etc.

I asked my clients if they wanted to participate in the "Wish List" and with their consent, I began keeping such a list. The participants told their loved ones that this "Wish List" existed at the spa. And from that day on, I became the go-to source of gifts for these special occasions. Men, in particular, were thrilled that they no longer had to struggle with getting the right gift and they were especially happy to know that the specifics of the gift would be a surprise to her.

The only caveat is that you must update the list regularly because there will be changes to your service menu, your product lineup and the gifts you have in stock. Even more importantly, your clients' favorites may change over the years as you bring in new products and services, so your Wish List must always be accurate.

Flyers and Announcements. Here is another one of those "studies show" factoids which is that if you want people to respond to something you are advertising, they must be exposed to it a minimum of five times. This means if you are trying to promote a seasonal service in your spa, you need to post it in five different places.

To determine what the five places will be, you must surreptitiously watch your clients and figure out where they look. For example, when they are waiting at the front desk to pay for their service, where do their eyes go? Are they looking straight ahead at whatever picture is on the wall? Are they looking at the retail displays? What is in their sightline when they are sitting in your waiting room prior to their appointment? Wherever they most often look is where a flyer should go.

Here is an obvious one: When they are sitting on the potty, is there a door or a wall in front of them? A captive audience...what a perfect spot for a flyer! When they are washing their hands, a flyer on the wall or mirror over the sink or paper towel holder is a great spot.

Because it takes five views before information absorbs, it's important to change your visual marketing materials often. Change the flyer every 4 to 6 weeks, or as often as most of your clients come in for services. Although the message can remain the same, you want them to view something different each time they come in. Otherwise they are going to get bored, and they will stop looking at whatever is posted. It needs to draw them in every time they see it.

Gift Cards and Gift Certificates. I know it can be especially exciting around the holidays when lots of gift certificates and gift cards are being sold. You see all that money coming in and you are ecstatic. But remember, there are federal and state laws related to gift cards and gift certificates, and there are a few things you must consider:

- You have taken in all of this gift card money, however, the services have not yet been provided. What happens if you close your business? Are you going to contact all the purchasers of these outstanding gift cards and make arrangements to provide the services before you close? Alternatively, can you afford to reimburse all these gift card holders? Because technically (and often legally), that money doesn't belong to you until the service has been provided.
- What if you sell your business? You are the one who took in this money. When the recipient wants to redeem their gift card, are you expecting the new owner to provide the outstanding services for free? Or will you pay the new owner the total dollar amount of the outstanding gift cards, even if there is a chance that some of them will never be redeemed?

I went through this when I sold my spa and let me tell you, it was not fun. But I learned an important lesson, so when I opened my new solo esthetics practice after selling my spa, I no longer offered gift certificates. I do not believe that the foundation of an esthetics practice should be built on gift certificates and gift cards.

MARKETING YOURSELF

Now you know all about how to market your business, but let us not forget that ultimately YOU are your business. Which means that some marketing of yourself will be required. Therefore, this is a good time to pull out your "Crazy Old Aunt in the Attic" list from Chapter 1 and review everything you have written so far.

Throughout this book, you have acquired several tools, tips, and strategies with which you can now create the esthetics business of your dreams. Hopefully, you can see clearly that those self-critical comments and that nagging voice are no longer needed.

So, my fellow Estheticians, the time has come to LET THAT GO! Unburden yourself. You have knowledge and clarity now that you may not have had previously. It is time to throw away the list, shred it, burn it, or whatever method will set you free and move you forward from your newly-created starting point. You've got this!

ME, MYSELF AND I

In this section, we will go over various ways to connect with potential clients, such as indirectly, like through your website and business cards; and directly, when you are out in the world being your fabulous self.

I know marketing is not anyone's favorite subject, but you must know how to market yourself because you <u>are</u> your esthetics business. That does not mean you have to "sell" yourself or talk people into liking you. This process can actually be fun, and it can happen organically with very little effort.

Do not allow fear to get in the way of your success, although do recognize that fear is actually a good thing in many ways. Fear forces us to hit pause sometimes and carefully consider decisions we are about to make, and that ultimately enables us to make better decisions. For example, fear is what makes us pause to look both ways before crossing a street. And after we have assessed the situation, we continue across the street because we want to get to the other side….alive. So fear can be present, but we get to choose just how much power it has over us.

Be Yourself. Nobody is exactly like you so nobody's career will be exactly like yours. Some see this career as being a part of the "beauty" business while others see it as a "clinical" career. And both would be correct. So use your instincts, be yourself, and follow your own dreams.

You may not realize it yet, but potential clients are all around you. Every time you are in a social situation, whether it is at church, a party, a meeting, or any gathering (especially with women in attendance), you are only an arm's length away from potential new clients.

That said, I am not suggesting you attempt to give a sales pitch to anyone, ever. (In fact, please don't do that!) I am simply suggesting that you become as knowledgeable and eloquent as you possibly can with all things related to skin care in general and also your esthetics specialty.

In my experience, the moment somebody realizes that I am an Esthetician, the conversation immediately turns to skin care. They want to ask questions about products, wrinkles, hyperpigmentation or perhaps their child's acne. This has happened so often in my esthetics career that it is usually me who veers the conversation away from skin care, because otherwise it would go on endlessly.

You must prepare yourself to talk about skin care on a moment's notice because when you are prepared, you will be confident and fear-less. You will be ready to put on your Professional Esthetician's hat and share your knowledge with anyone who is interested in skin care.

So my fellow Estheticians, go out into the world with your energy balanced, your head held high and your crown on straight, and enjoy being your magnificent self. Have your website and social media profiles ready, and always have your business cards with you so you can give them to anyone who is interested.

Business Card. When it comes to this important and very common marketing tool, never do what everyone else is doing. And that means do not waste the priority space on your business card by providing only your name and phone number. Instead, give them the more essential info on the front of your card, and use the back side for the address and phone number. Yes, it will cost a little more to print on the back side, however, not having to scrunch everything on the front and therefore having more space for important info is worth the extra cost.

As an example, here is what is on my Esthetician business card:

FRONT of card (the prime real estate):

- **Diane Buccola**
- **Esthetician**
- **NCEA Certified**

The viewer may not know what "NCEA Certified" means but it sounds impressive and it's different than most other Estheticians' business cards. If they are curious to know what "NCEA Certified" means, they can ask me (which gives me an opening to talk skin care with them) or they can do an internet search.

CA license number #####
Date I was licensed: **1999**

The next line can be a descriptor. Here are two examples:

1. Completely Customized Facials
2. Specializing in Clinical Esthetics

Those are the things that will pique their interest which will then result in them turning the card over to look for your contact info.

Here is what they will find on the BACK of the card:

- Address
- Phone
- Email
- Website

Doing it this way gives the potential client so much more pertinent information about you and your esthetics business. They now have everything they need to contact you, schedule an appointment, or go to your website where they can learn even more about you. You are properly utilizing this essential tool to market yourself organically, without having to sell yourself. Your business card does all the work for you!

A WEBSITE IS MANDATORY

Even if you are not particularly internet savvy, you must have a website. This applies to all Estheticians whether they are an employee or self-employed. People of all ages and income levels are seeking information online, therefore, you need an online presence.

There are many user-friendly and inexpensive build-your-own websites which you can create and manage yourself if you do not care to invest in a highly-technical website. All that is really required is basic information, such as your contact info, hours of operation, menu, and some information about who you are. The most important information – such as what makes you and your services special -- needs to be on your landing page. If they like what they see there, they will continue to explore your site and will look for your contact info.

Landing Page. Your website does not have to be fancy or expensive, but it must have a landing page that provides your message in a clear and concise way. If you are not familiar with the term "landing page," it simply just means the page a visitor will see when they follow a link and "land" at your website.

Your Message. If you meet a potential client somewhere or if somebody refers a friend to you, the first thing they are going to do is search for you online. For that reason, it is imperative that you put some thought into what you want your message to be. For example, if you are marketing your esthetics business and hoping potential clients will schedule an appointment with you, then that should be the focus of your landing page.

Your message is far more important than having some big fancy logo, glamour shots of yourself, or your contact information all over the front page. If a visitor to your site is interested in what they see on your landing page, they will scroll down to find your contact info. However, if the first and most prominent thing they see is your contact info, they may not scroll any further.

Keep in mind, simply giving facials does not necessarily make you stand out...because all Estheticians give facials. For that reason, you must provide information that is more specific. You need to tell a story. Perhaps it is an explanation of your skin care philosophy, your background, or what you love about esthetics. Anything that gives the viewer an idea of who you are (not just what you do) and tells them why they might want to schedule an appointment with you.

You can tell your story in a variety of ways. One is to upload a photo of yourself, perhaps wearing your lab coat, or if you think your treatment room or waiting area is special, show that too. Be sure to add text that tells your story.

Another option is to create a video for your landing page which is easy to do on your smart phone. Personally, I think videos are best because the viewer can see you and hear you and feel like they somewhat know you.

No matter how you do this, be sure you include an invitation or what is known as a "Call to Action." You want the viewer to do something, to take action, to contact you or schedule an appointment. You must spell it out, invite them in. Offer a free brief consultation. Tell them about your VIP program, mention lots of free parking, evening appointments… whatever will answer the all-important question: What's in it for me?

End with something like, "Here is my phone number (or "my phone number is below"). Please be sure to ask for me by name…." In other words, tell them what you want them to do!

If we magnified our successes as much as we magnify our disappointments, we'd all be much happier.
~Abraham Lincoln

7 SERVICES

Consultation + Fee

Estheticians will offer various types of consultations for clients and potential clients. Some will be at no charge and others will involve a fee. This VIP consultation will be reserved for potential new clients, and the length will be 20 to 30 minutes. A fee definitely will be charged. Of course, you can charge whatever you want to depending upon how detailed you want this consultation to be, however for purposes of this example, I am suggesting a fee somewhere in the vicinity of $20-$50.

This fee-based consultation is intended for serious clients, those who make an appointment and come to your place of business. What they will receive is all your time and attention as you teach them about their skin and how to properly care for it. But the true purpose of this appointment is to introduce yourself, your facility, and your service menu, as well as to explain your esthetics training, your education, and your credentials.

It is advantageous to have visual aids available to share with your new client during this consultation; for example, a skin scanner or Woods Lamp, and possibly a moisture checker. Posters are great aids as well so you can teach the client about the skin's epidermal layers.

You can use the consultation fee as impetus for the client to schedule a facial or buy products by simply advising them that 100% of the consultation fee can go towards their first facial or any products purchased that day.

Customized Facials

We need to keep up with the times and be in touch with the needs of our demographic. Therefore, a lengthy facial menu may not be serving you well. As clients veer away from pricey treatments offered by dermatologists, they are looking to Estheticians to provide clinical facial services. This is not to imply that you can't also have a relaxing facial or two, but you should incorporate into your menu facial treatments that are customized to fit the specific needs of your clientele, which may be more than a feel-good facial.

When I went from a spa owner to a Solo Esthetician, I changed things to suit my independent status. I got rid of a traditional facial menu and went to complete customization. As a Solo Esthetician, I had only two facials on my menu. One I called "Bells & Whistles" (B&W) which meant it including everything; hand treatment, eye treatment, and a variety of esthetic electrical equipment.

The other facial was just a Basic Facial, and the reason for having the Basic Facial on the menu was simply to offer clients a lower-priced option. However, every time I had a new client coming in, I treated them to the B&W Facial, but I only charged them the price of the Basic Facial. That way, they got to experience the B&W Facial without having to pay the higher price.

My hope was that having enjoyed all the fabulous perks of the B&W Facial, in the future they would want to stick with the higher-priced facial, only now they would be paying full price. And that is exactly what happened. Not once did anyone ever request the Basic Facial.

Maintenance (VIP) prices

One really great way to ensure prompt rebookings and prevent no-shows is to offer two-tiered pricing. What this means is that if a client rebooks or schedules a series of appointments in advance, they will pay a slightly lower rate.

Here's how it works:

Let's say your price for a lip wax is $25, and your lip wax clients typically come in every 4 weeks. To take advantage of the VIP program, your clients must schedule their next appointment <u>as they are leaving their current appointment</u>, and that next appointment must be within your required 4-week timeframe.

If the client keeps that next appointment as scheduled, she will pay a discounted rate of $20 for the lip wax service, which saves her $5. If, however, she does not keep that appointment or she reschedules to a time outside the required 4-week timeframe, then the regular $25 price will apply.

This can also work with facials. Maintenance pricing would be $10 or $20 lower, depending upon the regular price of your facials.

I know technically this is a "maintenance" program rather than a VIP program, but who doesn't want to feel like a VIP? Being identified and treated as a VIP may be the thing that encourages the client to participate in the program.

SPECIALITY DEMOGRAPHICS

As was mentioned in an earlier chapter, the barometer for success in the esthetics business is based upon the lives of women. This means we must be ever mindful of women's esthetics needs, as well as their personal needs, and be willing to change with the times.

There are many reasons today's women may not want to come in for a regular monthly facial. If you add up driving time, time to change out of their clothes before the facial and time to change back into their clothes after the facial, an hour facial is actually much longer than an hour. It is not only about the time involved for the facial itself, but it's also about what I call "post-facial recovery" time which refers to the fact that some women are uncomfortable going directly from the facial room to anywhere they will be out in public.

This means they either must go home and stay there or go home and fix themselves up before resuming their day. This is an obstacle we should remove to make it easier for our female clients. For these reasons, it is easy to understand that not every woman can fit a monthly facial into her schedule. But it definitely does not mean that really good skin care and great advice from a licensed Esthetician is not necessary or not possible.

What women <u>want</u> is skin care advice from a professional. That is what they are looking for online and in department stores. But what women <u>need</u> is access to an Esthetician. If they meet with an Esthetician, they will be able to understand their skin and how to take care of it properly.

So, let's work with these women. If you do not already have a facial service designed to accommodate the lives of today's busy women, you are missing out on a lucrative source of revenue.

The grass is always greener where you water it.
~Neil Barringham

ABBREVIATED SERVICES

Let's add facial services that will allow busy women to have a facial and get on a really good home care regimen. This type of facial would be streamlined, which may require elimination of certain elements of a traditional facial, such as the massage. Products we choose for this service would take into consideration her need to go effortlessly on with her day once she leaves your facial room. An example would be utilizing a lift-off mask that does not require removal with water.

If you offer makeup services, a sure-fire upsell would be a 10-minute daytime makeup application. Alternatively, you can allow her to use your makeup samples and testers, assuming you provide disposable tools for her use. If you have a dedicated area where she can apply her own makeup, that would be a major perk for women who may have to go directly from their facial to another appointment, or back to work...or anyplace besides back home.

Any of these scenarios opens the door to the possibility of makeup sales, so it is a win-win.

The Name. I do not recommend calling this abbreviated facial a "Mini Facial." In fact, I suggest we get away from the name "mini facial" entirely. People already have an idea of what they think a mini-facial is so when that name appears on your menu, they already have a specific expectation. Additionally, the term "mini-facial" has been around a long time which makes it rather stale and boring today.

The service I am suggesting is a full facial, it is not a "mini" facial. Just because a client does not have to change into a facial wrap, and perhaps the mask is quicker, does not mean it is not a full facial. So name it something fun like "Glow-on-the-Go!" Or use skin-specific serums and name it "Targeted Facial Infusion." Whatever you call it, be sure the benefits of the facial are made clear to clients and potential clients. Remember to always keep in mind the client's all-important question: "What's in it for me?"

Many "Minis"

When it comes to abbreviated facials, there are so many name options beyond "mini facial." Here are some of my ideas, which you are welcome to use.

- Consultations & follow-ups
- Mini Delights
- A la Carte
- Spa Tapas
- Small Bites/Bytes
- Spot Treatments
- Targeted/Focused

The reason I picked the names listed here is because these are names I've seen, and because people who are looking at these names will know immediately that it means "smaller" or "quicker." My favorite is "Targeted/Focused" which in my esthetics business meant an exfoliation and serum infusion. Easy and fast.

Multiple small visits = increased profit. It is actually quite fun to do these quickie treatments because not only will this provide you with multiple breaks during your work day, but you will also see more clients. Even though you might prefer that all clients have full-length facials, when you add up multiple clients having abbreviated facials and purchasing home care products from you, it adds up to big profit.

Power Hour

Here is another way to add an abbreviated service to your menu. I have named it "Power Hour" but it doesn't have to be an hour and it doesn't have to be called "power hour." Some might recognize this name as typically referring to a lunchtime peel, but it doesn't have to happen at lunch and it doesn't have to be a peel.

Power Hour facials will not fall into the clinical facial category, therefore the intake process can be brief. As mentioned above, skip the facial wrap and the hair wrap, if possible.

Choose fun names so these facials will set themselves apart from your longer full facial services. For example, "30-minute Glow" tells the prospective client that this is a 30-minute service. Busy professionals may not realize these shorter services are available which will easily fit into their busy workday. When assessing this service, their thought will be: "Oh, this is only 30 minutes...I can do this!"

Look at the big picture here. This is not only about facials and products. This is a great opportunity to get people into your facility who may not otherwise come in for a full facial. This marketing strategy will give them a chance to meet you and your staff, as well as view your full menu. Odds are very high that they will consider having a full facial with you sometime in the future. This could very well be the start of a whole new clientele for you.

SPECIALTY DEMOGRAPHICS

In an earlier chapter I talked about typical demographics...the ones you are already familiar with. The list below, however, is about specialty demographics; in other words, a group of people in your area that you can appeal to based upon specific services.

Very few changes to your menu and product lineup are necessary to curate services that would apply to these specialty demographics. This is simply about identifying groups of potential clients and marketing to them. The focus and goal of your marketing strategy to cultivate these potential clients is simply to encourage the target customer to recognize himself or herself.

- Women over 60 (or 50, 40, etc.)
- Men with beards
- Vegan
- Actors/theaters (heavy makeup)
- Surfers (sun exposure, salt water)
- Humid locations
- High altitude
- Swimmers (chlorinated water)
- Locally sourced products
- Environmentally friendly products and services
- Face yoga/aerobics
- School age services

"Mature" Skin. Of course, many Estheticians offer services for "mature skin" but what does that really mean? Generally speaking, that could mean anything. However, if you narrow your niche to offer skin care services for "women over 60, the women who relate to this category will think, "Oh, wow, that's me! I am a woman and I'm over 60. This Esthetician knows exactly what I need!" Some women in this demographic may not understand how or why their skin is changing, so they won't know what to do about it, and they don't know what they need. Being a specialist in this area could be a lucrative niche for an Esthetician.

Men with beards. Those of us who have male clients will occasionally deal with bearded men, and that is a whole different service than a facial service for clean shaven male faces. Estheticians cannot perform every element of a traditional facial with this demographic, so adjustments must be made to accommodate a bearded face. A man with a beard learning of this service would recognize himself and think "Oh, wow, that's me. I can get a facial even though I have a beard."

Vegan. These days you can easily find vegan products and supplies, and our vegan friends would love to know their preferences are acknowledged and that there are esthetics services within their comfort zone.

Actors and theater people. These people are under lights and are often using heavy makeup for long periods of time. They could certainly use guidance, products and services from a Professional Esthetician in their area.

Surfers. I added this one because I live near the beach and there are surfers around me often. They deal with sun exposure and salt water which, as Professional Estheticians know, will affect the skin.

Humid locations. It is fascinating what weather can do to the skin. What works for someone in a dry climate does not always work for those in a humid climate. Client's needs will vary and their products must accommodate the variations. Humidity may require products that are lighter in weight, definitely less rich and heavy, or perhaps oil free. And for those traveling to a humid climate, you might consider offering travel size humidity-friendly products.

High altitude. A weekend in the mountains can completely change the appearance of your skin. You might look in the mirror and find someone 10 years older looking back at you! Of course, when you go back home, your skin returns to normal. But for someone who lives in high altitude 24/7, that's a whole different thing. These clients need specific services and home care products.

Swimmers. Whether these are recreational swimmers, college swimmers or competitive swimmers, this demographic is dealing with sun, sunscreen, and chlorinated water. There is much a Professional Esthetician can do for this group.

Locally sourced. If there is a particular ingredient grown in your area, such as lavender or citrus, you could incorporate that into your product line and your services. You could become a locally-sourced product and facial service expert.

Environmentally friendly. So much of what you use in your treatment room can be environmentally friendly such as packaging, products, sheets on your bed, etc. This effort would warm the hearts of this demographic.

Face Yoga. Yoga is very popular so using that word will grab the attention of many yoga devotees. There is such a thing as Face Yoga, and you can incorporate certain elements into the facial massage portion of your facial service.

RETAIL-ONLY

Some say that in our business, retail is king/queen, and that is a true statement. Retail sales are important and should be very profitable for you. However, as a Professional Esthetician, you never want to sell products to anyone who has not had a comprehensive consultation with you first.

Ideally, we would love to have all clients come in for regular monthly facials. But realistically, that is never going to happen. This means that far too many women are purchasing products from drug stores, department stores, TV ads, and Multi-Level-Marketing companies. Clearly, these women need our help!

When you are out in the world meeting people and marketing yourself, do not make the mistake of neglecting those women whom you believe may not become regularly monthly facial clients. It is precisely this type of woman (or man) who could potentially become your annual or semi-annual client...that is, if you are willing to expand your services to accommodate them.

Perhaps these clients would be willing to come in for an annual diagnostic facial, followed by a home care protocol recommendation; and they will follow this protocol with those products until their next annual facial. It is certainly better to have them using your high-quality professional home care products than it would be for them to be using over-the-counter, over-priced and low-quality products.

"RETAIL-ONLY" CLIENTS

This category of client stems from a relatively new development that has arisen because of the internet. And when I say "new" development, I am referencing those of us who began our esthetics career before the internet came on the scene. The advent of the internet was a game changer for us.

Everything you can touch today, at some point did not exist until somebody took an idea all the way to the end.

Who knows why some women do not want to have a regular facial? It could be a comfort issue or a privacy issue. It could be a result of their financial situation, time constraints, or health concerns. The list is endless, and it is not our business to know their reasons. Whatever the reason may be, these women still want great skin. but without the guidance of a Professional Esthetician, they are going to end up with bad info, lousy products, and unmet goals.

So let's not neglect these clients. Let's instead find a way to work with them. But, first, a few important rules:

A Professional Esthetician does NOT sell products to anyone who has not previously had a consultation. This doesn't mean these clients are required to have regular monthly facials, but they must at the very least have met with us prior to purchasing professional skin care products.

We must make it easy for clients to replenish their products. Free shipping or personal delivery is a great way to do that. I have been known to drop products off at someone's doorstep if they live nearby or take the products to my child's school and deliver to my client's car when we are picking up our kids. It is a nice gesture and if it is convenient for you, why not do it? This qualifies as stellar customer service.

Although our "Retail-Only Clients" may not fit the traditional role of a typical facial client, keep in mind that these clients are buying retail from you, and they are not taking up any treatment room space, nor are they taking up any of your time. In fact, they are not costing you anything at all. It is simply sales of retail products done the right way by a Professional Esthetician. A new, and potentially very lucrative, concept worth embracing.

"RETAIL-ONLY" APPOINTMENTS

Consultation Appointment

Again, no selling professional products to anybody unless they have come in to see you for a consultation first. They must have some type of introductory appointment with you. Here is an idea of what I mean by "introductory appointment."

This appointment is 30-45 minutes (or whatever you want it to be). It is simple and it is easy. There is no facial gown, there is no head wrap, and there is no facial. This is an "analyze/intake form/educate" appointment.

You can charge whatever you want, a starting point might be $1.50 to $2 per minute. At your discretion, the fee for this appointment may be waived if they put it towards purchase of home care retail. Typically, this offer is too hard for a prospective client to pass up so they probably will purchase products.

If they do purchase products, it is mandatory they leave this appointment with a written home care protocol so they know exactly how to use each product they have purchased. If they do not use the products properly, they will not reach their skin care goals, and they will not be impressed with you.

Check-in Appointments

Since you are not seeing your Retail-Only Clients for regular facials, you must be able to get them in at least briefly to keep them on the right path with their home care products and protocols. It will be up to you to determine how often you want to see these clients, but whenever they do come in for these check-in appointments, it must be a simple and easy service. This appointment should be about evaluation, education, introduction of new products (in other words, just informational). Your ultimate goal as their Esthetician is to adjust their home care protocols, if necessary, and to assist them with replenishment of their home care products.

During check-in appointments, begin by reviewing their home care products. I suggest you tweak something (if there is something to tweak) so they see that you know what you are doing and that it is wise for them to rely on your guidance. For example, if the season or the weather has changed, or perhaps the condition of their skin has changed, you might want to change the serum or the moisturizer, or add a sunscreen, etc.

Same thing with their home care protocol if there is something that needs to be added, removed, or changed. For example, if they are using Retinol at night during the winter but now the weather has changed and it is sunny and hot, this would be the perfect time to change their method of exfoliation.

Annual/Semi-annual Appointments

I highly recommend that you have your Retail-Only Clients come in once a year, every six months, or quarterly, for some sort of in-person facial experience. By now, these clients will be familiar with your home care retail products, they will be feeling comfortable with you, and they will be very happy with their skin. These clients are now ready for a full facial -- or at least an abbreviated facial service. This means that what began as a Retail-Only Client could very well become a regular, loyal, long-term monthly facial client.

E-STORE

Password-protected Shopping Page: As mentioned earlier, it is essential that you make it easy for your regular clients and your

Retail-Only Clients to purchase products from you, so you definitely want to have an e-store...but it must be a password-protected e-store. Every website builder software has this option, so setting it up is simple.

On your website's landing page, it should be made clear that you are a trained and licensed Professional Esthetician and that anybody you sell products to must have a consultation prior to purchase.

It should also be pointed out that you guarantee your products are fresh, that they are stored properly, and that as a licensed Professional Esthetician, you are trained to know which products will be best for each skin condition. Mention that skin conditions change regularly for various reasons such as changes in weather, hormones, lifestyle, etc., and you are trained to deal with those variables.

Posting the Product Diversion information that I referred to in an earlier chapter would be a great idea. If you have decided to go with no shipping fees, then definitely mention that too. This is the sort of information that will entice potential clients to read further. This is much better use of your landing page than simply posting your service menu. If they like what they are reading about you and your esthetics practice, they will scroll down and/or follow links to other pages.

Once Retail-Only Clients have been through your initial consultation process, then you can refer them to your password-protected (client-only) shopping page.

I suggest you consider changing your shopping page's password regularly, such as every 6 months, at least. You must keep an eye on who is purchasing and who is coming in for check-in appointments. That way, when you change the password, you'll know who to send the new password to. You do not want to send the new password to everyone because someone who came in for a consultation 5 years ago could still have access to your products even though they have never been back. And even worse, they could share that password with others.

Changing the password regularly also gives you a good excuse to reconnect with your Retail-Only Clients because you must give them the new password. At that point, you can inquire about how the products are working for them, ask if they would like to come in for a facial service, and you can tell them about any new products or services.

Random product sales is not the path to becoming financially successful. It is the path to becoming a struggling salesperson.

HOLIDAY PARTIES

Where it all began….

I told you in an earlier chapter about my family's women's clothing stores where I worked throughout my teens and early 20s. This is where I first got the idea about annual holiday parties which I eventually adapted to fit my spa.

To give you a little background on the origin of this annual event, my family owned four stores, and we held an annual Gentlemen's Christmas Party at the flagship store which was inside an indoor shopping mall. All the men connected to the female clients from all four of our stores were invited to the event.

The party was held in the evening when the mall was closed so we had the run of the place. There was food and drinks and lots of men. All of our sales staff was there, including me. Our job was to assist the gentlemen as they chose Christmas gifts for the women in their life. The men ate, drank, partied, shopped, and then departed.

Later we would wrap the gifts and have them delivered to the gentleman's home or place of business. This event went on successfully for 20 years, and it is that experience that prompted me to create the Ladies' Holiday Party for my spa, and later the Gentlemen's Holiday Party. Of course, elements from both of the parties suggested below can be combined for a co-ed party.

LADIES HOLIDAY PARTY

I adapted the men's night idea to fit my spa and the result became "Ladies Night." This annual event turned out to be very successful for me and if you'd like to give it a try, here are the details:

Choose an evening or weekend afternoon – whatever will work best for the majority of your clients – and throw a get-together at your spa

169

or studio. If your location is small, make it an Open House so that your guests' arrival times will vary.

Calendar. With women, you should plan a little further ahead than you might for men. 30 days ahead is not too far in advance to throw this girls' holiday shindig. Just be sure you have thought this through well in advance and have ordered your Christmas and holiday retail accordingly.

Food. Provide some easy appetizers. In my experience, women do not usually eat much, so there is no need to go overboard. Serve hot tea, or wine if that is legal in your area. Keep in mind that serving alcohol will increase your expenses by quite a bit, and those partaking of alcoholic beverages will likely stay longer. However, that does not necessarily translate to those guests purchasing anything. In fact, the opposite could be true. They may just stick around and enjoy the free beverages. (If you do serve alcohol, be sure you are following the laws and rules in your area.)

Mini Services. Offer whatever easy services you can, such as chair massage, hand massage, heated hand mitt treatments, and eye mask treatments.

Program. Have a printed program setting out the events and opportunities of the evening (sale, mini services, to-go gifts, gift wrap, gift certificates). It is a great way to get your name and menu in your guests' hands.

Sale Table. This is a great time to have a "sale" table with discounted products that you'd like to get rid of, provided they still have a suitable shelf life remaining. Have your holiday gift items wrapped and displayed very prominently in the room so your clients can follow their impulsive shopping instincts.

Stocking Stuffers. Always keep stocking stuffers in mind such as little things that clients will buy as hostess gifts for holiday parties, or to serve as gifts to teachers, holiday gift exchanges, and other holiday events.

Help. This is super important! Be certain to bring somebody in to help you with this event. You will be wearing many hats at this event: Salesperson, cashier, marketing executive, concierge, Esthetician and janitor. It's a good idea to have somebody there to help, or by the end of the event you will feel that you did not pay enough attention to many of your guests. Remember, your guests will not necessarily know each other because usually they are coming in at separate times for their appointments. It is best for you to be the hostess while somebody else helps out with tasks such as processing payments, wrapping gifts, pouring beverages, etc. Even if you must pay somebody a couple of hours wages, it will be worth it.

Music. Do not rely on the same old Christmas music because by the time your event rolls around, people have probably been hearing it since Halloween. Instead choose upbeat music, because studies show livelier music will result in people buying more items and doing it faster.

Sample Bar. If you are able to provide a hands-on sample bar so party guests can touch, smell and bond with the products, that is a wonderful idea. Keep in mind, this event is not only about buying products for Christmas. It is about getting people into your spa, introducing them to your business, showing off your treatment room and presenting yourself in a positive light.

GENTLEMEN'S HOLIDAY EVENT

Historically, men are last-minute holiday shoppers. While they probably know that the women in their lives love facials and massage and other spa services, they do not necessarily completely understand the ritual and/or the purpose. We must make it easy for them to give their business to us, which means we want them to feel comfortable walking into our spa or esthetics business.

For purposes of this explanation, I will be using the term "Christmas" because that is the holiday that applied to my business. However, this applies to any holiday that you or your clients will be celebrating.

The calendar. I suggest picking one night, preferably a week or two before Christmas, and hold a Men's Shopping Night. You should hold this event before Christmas obviously – before the men have already done their Christmas shopping, but not so far in advance that men's brains are not yet in holiday mode.

Invite. Advertise the event by way of newspaper ad or mailers if you want to invite the general public. Alternatively, you can send holiday-themed postcards to clients' homes if you prefer to keep it exclusive.

Food and drink. You can make this a big event by offering food and drink. Or you can simply offer a hot drink and a shopping bag for the men to fill. Men typically do not enjoy the shopping experience as much as women do, so plan accordingly.

Manly. Always try to make things easy for the men who may have never previously stepped into a spa or esthetics business. If you are hoping to gain male facial clients, then do what you can to get rid of the girly decorations for the evening so that it feels a bit more gentlemen friendly.

Put up signs advertising your Gentlemen's services. And if you do not already have men's services on your menu, create some. Place your men's products front and center and have testers available so men can feel and smell the products while they are there.

You need a man. If you have a brother, son, boyfriend, husband or male friend, bring him in to assist you that night, even if it is simply as a greeter. Men will feel more comfortable in a spa or esthetics business if they are not the only man in the room. The more comfortable they feel, the more likely they will linger longer which will translate into more purchases and a better rapport.

Ready-to-go. Do whatever you can to make the gifts grab-and-go. (This is not just true for men, this is the way to attract all holiday shoppers who tend to buy on impulse.) Most men who are shopping for women want to get in, make their purchase, and get out. Be sure gifts, gift cards and gift certificates are beautifully packaged because if he must wrap it himself, he may not come back next year. And of course, make a note of what each male shopper bought so that you can put it on your client's "Wish List" and refer to it next year.

Wrap it up. It is vital that your holiday items are gift-wrapped or that you can wrap them quickly. Even if you do not usually offer gift wrapping, 'tis the season to change the rules. At the very least, buy some bags at your local wholesale florist/gift supply, along with some holiday tissue.

You can make gift cards and gift certificates special by purchasing holiday-themed envelopes at your local office supply to package gift cards and gift certificates. Make an impact whenever you can because word-of-mouth is your best advertisement.

Men are very loyal customers, and once your Gentlemen's Holiday Evening becomes well-known, it will grow to be an annual event that everyone looks forward to and depends upon.

Other Party Themes. You can throw a shindig any time of year with varying themes. How about a Summer Tropical party? Play Hawaiian music, serve tropical drinks, highlight your sunscreen and other summer products and, of course, your Tantalizing Tropical Treatments. This is a great way to showcase your sandal-worthy foot treatments, if you have any.

The same thing can be done during winter by highlighting your Warm Winter Treatments and hydrating products.

Sometimes life is about risking everything
for a dream that nobody else can see.

8 **YOUR SPACE**

Choosing a space within which to set up your esthetics practice is exciting, but there can be obstacles and pitfalls. There are things to look for and there are things to avoid. I know this because I have done it. More than once, actually. Most things went okay for me because I had some really good advice, which I am going to pass along to you. But there are elements you should consider before you start looking for a space.

I will take you through my experience so that when it is your turn, you can hopefully avoid some of my mistakes. That way, you will be a few steps ahead in the process of choosing, and using, your esthetics space.

LOCATION

When it comes to location, here are five things that I think deserve careful consideration:

Neighborhood. You want to choose a neighborhood that is convenient for you of course, but it would be wise to also assess the type of neighbors that surround you. Do they fit the profile of your preferred demographic? Before you can answer this question, you must decide who you want to be in esthetics and what will be your brand. Once you have decided that, then you can determine the type

175

of clients you want to attract. Once you have that client profile in mind, you are ready to find the perfect location for your esthetics business.

Noise. It can be difficult to determine if noise will be a problem when you have spent only a short time inside a potential location as you visit various spaces for rent or lease. While it is a safe bet that sharing a wall with a restaurant, bar, karate studio, or exercise venue will produce disruptive noise, others might not be so obvious. For example, road noise and parking activity may be sporadic and harder to assess depending on time of day. But we need to be sure that nothing external will ruin the tranquil environment of an esthetics space.

Competition. You should consider what businesses surround your space, but there is no need to worry too much about the competition other than to assess what they are doing and what they are not doing. It helps to learn what products competing businesses are using and selling because you definitely do not want to duplicate that. But unless your goal is to have a "walk-in" esthetics business, you don't have to worry about competition. Clients do not choose an Esthetician based entirely upon what the business looks like from the outside, or where it is located. Their choice is primarily based upon how they are treated and how they feel when they are in your space.

Accessibility. This has to do with easy and free parking, if that is applicable to your city and your location. Some people will choose not to do business with places where they have to worry about moving their car in an hour or having to pay for parking. Stairs is another issue. If your location is not on the ground floor, or there is no elevator, you must consider how that might limit your potential client pool. We must make it as easy as possible for people to come to us, which translates into making it easy for them spend their money with us.

Utilities. You must confirm that the space you are considering has all the utilities you will need for your business, and you should be sure everything is in working condition. Assuming you will have sinks in the treatment rooms, you must check the plumbing situation. You will need hot water, so be sure to confirm the water heater has the capacity you will require. You should know the location of electrical outlets and whether they will be suitable for your power cords. (Be mindful of whether there are laws that dictate which type of power cords are required to run your electrical equipment.)

Perhaps you will have a washer and dryer in your space, which could require either gas or electricity. You may live in an area where air conditioning matters, so you should confirm that is available. You should assess the current condition of all these elements, and you should confirm who pays for them, and most importantly who is responsible for the repair if and when they fail.

CHECKLIST FOR OWNERS

If you find a space you like, there are many things to consider before you sign on the dotted line. For example, the odds of you finding a space that is set up perfectly for your needs are slim, so you might have to do some tenant improvements which may involve construction. If that is the case, depending upon how much construction you must do, you may then be dealing with permits and inspections.

Depending upon your State, County and City rules, you may need specific licensing such as a business license. In California, we also must have an Establishment License, which may be called something else in other states. You will need to check with your County and whichever licensing board oversees your Esthetician license because they could have rules you must adhere to such as zoning restrictions.

You might be required to alter things in order to comply with ADA rules (Americans with Disabilities Act). In other words, your space may require handicapped accessibility; for example, doorways may have to be a certain width, with door handles of a certain type, or special equipment may have to be installed in the bathroom.

If you are planning to hire other Estheticians or technicians, you will need to know the difference between an Independent Contractor and an Employee. These are IRS rules which means it is Federal law, so you really do need to understand the distinction between the two classifications. (This topic will be discussed in more detail in the next chapter.)

If you plan to have employees, you must become familiar with Federal and State Labor Laws. I had to fire somebody once, and fortunately I am a really good record keeper, so I was prepared for the pushback.

Insurance. By now, everybody understands that Estheticians must have liability insurance, but as owners of businesses and lessees of space, we must also consider potential issues such as damage to windows, roof leaks, and other property damage. You must confirm who will have to pay for that. Is that something you might be responsible for? If so, you should have property damage insurance, in addition to liability insurance.

GETTING NOTICED

It is essential that you give some careful thought to exactly what sort of clientele you wish to develop. For example, will you rely on walk-in traffic? If so, you should be located where people are easily able to see your building and view your sign as they drive or walk by.

While being located on a busy street might be a good thing, if prospective clients are whizzing by in their cars, will they even notice you? And if your name is generic ("What's-Her-Name's Day Spa"), will they comprehend what sort of treatments you offer and what services you specialize in? Before committing to a location, think about how you would market yourself there.

My day spa was located on a busy street, and I used an old-fashioned sandwich board sign at the curb to get drivers' attention. It worked well for me, but if you are considering this marketing option, be sure to note the posted speed limit on the street, the direction of travel, and which way drivers will likely be looking as they pass by, because these elements could make or break a sandwich board strategy.

Also, be sure to check your City or County's regulations regarding sandwich board signs, as sometimes their location may be restricted, or they may be prohibited entirely.

My sign was remarkably simple, because there was not much time to grab the drivers' attention as they sped by. For that reason, my sandwich board sign was brief. It said simply: Facials-Massage-Waxing, at the top, followed by my company name and phone number.

I knew that drivers would not be able to ingest all the information in the few seconds they had to glance at my sign. But I also knew that if, at the very least, they saw the priority info which was "Facials-Massage-Waxing," they would know what services I offered and that is what mattered most..

I also knew odds were relatively high that they might also be able to recall the first word of my business name (which was "SKIN"), which meant they could look me up later. And even if they could remember nothing else, they knew where I was so if they were interested, they could circle back to get my contact info or stop in.

That marketing technique was very inexpensive yet extremely successful for me. However, if I would have put too much information on that sign, if the writing was too small, or if the name of the spa was too generic, it would have been a flop.

If you prefer to attract a younger crowd, locate yourself near their schools or colleges, or at least on a path to wherever else they might be going. If the 30s and 40s age group is attractive to you, find an elementary school, shopping center, or grocery store where moms will be.

If your goal is to be an upscale luxury spa or exclusive esthetics business, you might consider locations with a golf course or country club nearby. Whatever you choose, be sure to do a drive-by or walk-by at various times of day to assess the feasibility of the location(s) you are considering.

USING YOUR SPACE

Who do you want to be?

Another thing to ponder as you assess your location options is what you intend to do with your space. As mentioned earlier, not everybody needs to be a day spa, so do think very carefully about the services you will offer before you choose a space. Sadly, some day spas are struggling because they have not kept up with the lives of women.

No Need to be a Spa. I briefly entertained the idea of offering body treatments when I opened my day spa, however back then expensive equipment was a major part of "day spas" which meant I would have had to factor that into my budget. Fortunately, I took some great advice and inquired of people who were in my preferred client demographic before I purchased any equipment. To my surprise (and delight!), they all said they would only opt for the fancy body treatments if they were on vacation, or at a resort, because there they had more time to spend. But at home, they would have a facial, they would have a massage, they would want hair removal services, but very rarely would they have a body treatment. So I promptly abandoned that idea, and I am glad I did.

The Environment. Another reason not to be a traditional day spa is the environment. For example, nails and hair involve a lot of noise from equipment and conversation, and a lot of odors which are not always pleasant. Whereas massage and esthetics are typically quieter and smell nice. You do not want to blend those two environments, if you can help it.

If you are not adamant about offering all those services, then just don't do it. On the other hand, if you are committed to having all these services and being a "day spa," at least consider separating those two categories, if possible. Offer nail and hair services on one side and esthetics and massage services a good distance away.

Profitability. If producing the most amount of income is your priority, you must consider which services are the most profitable. If you are simply renting out rooms, you will have a static amount of money coming in, so this will not apply to you. However, do consider that by having booth renters, you lose out on a percentage of their service and sales income.

Low-profit. One example of a low profit-producing service is nail care. Yes, they will bring in repeat customers, but nail technicians do not have the opportunity for retail sales that your esthetics department does. You will likely find that your square footage will bring in quite a bit more profit if it is being used for esthetics services rather than nail care.

For purposes of providing you with a very general idea regarding how your various service areas compare to each other with regard to income, begin by calculating how much square footage each of your service departments take up. Take the number of square feet used by your esthetics department, and divide that number into the total income that department generates in a month. The resulting number is very generally your "income per square foot" for the esthetics department. (To calculate profit, you can figure in your costs of running each department, but for purposes of simplicity, I am not doing that here.)

You can use this formula to determine the income or profit from all the other departments in your spa and compare them with your esthetics department. Odds are that the per-foot income generated by your manicure and pedicure space or your massage room does not compare to the profit that comes from your facial room(s), simply because of the unique retail opportunities afforded by esthetic services.

No profit. And then there are some areas that produce absolutely no income at all. Of course, you need a few of these areas, but you can at least control how much space they occupy. Some of these spaces are large waiting rooms, staff break rooms and lockers. While it is a nice gesture to offer non-profitable services and spaces, unless your other more profitable services are providing the extra income to cover the income that is being lost, or you don't mind forfeiting the lost income, it may not be a wise choice for you.

Make the "most income per square foot" ratio a goal in your business. If you are devoting a lot of square footage to something that is not bringing you the income that you desire, get rid of it and instead use that space to expand another of your more profitable departments.

EMPLOYEE MANUAL

Do not skip this step if you have employees. I know the thought of creating an employee manual is nauseating, but it is vital to the happy environment of your esthetics business or spa. It takes some effort to prepare, but in the long run, it will save you a lot of time and a lot of trouble (including legal trouble).

Job description. The concept of an employee manual is simple: The owner will list every job description and the duties that apply to that position. You would do this in great detail beginning with what the person in that position is supposed to do when they arrive at their job, all the way through until they leave for the day.

For example, Receptionist: Arrive 15 minutes before we open, turn on all the lights, turn on the heater or air conditioning, light the candles, start the music, check bathroom supplies and replenish if needed, confirm next day's appointments by 10:00 am., etc.

When creating your Employee Manual, every job description should be listed even if the position is unfilled at the moment. Do not leave anything unclear because you cannot expect people to read your mind. Write it all down and give current employees a copy of the manual, and also present a copy to each new employee as you hire him or her.

Have each employee sign an acknowledgement form indicating that they have received a copy of the Employee Manual <u>and have read it</u>. If you ever have to fire an employee, you will have written evidence of any rules they were made aware of and perhaps have broken or disregarded which caused the termination of their employment.

In case of emergency. If any problems arise, employees will know exactly what to do and whom to call because it will be included in the Employee Manual. An example of situations you might want to include would be if a staff member or an Esthetician is going to be late arriving to work, whom do they call? Do they call you, the owner of the spa? Or do they call the manager? Or do they call another Esthetician to cover for them? And then who alerts the client of this change? Spell it all out in the Employee Manual.

The benefit. When creating your Employee Manual, include every detail that is important to you so everyone knows what to do and who does what. This will make management of employees so much easier, happier and more fun for everyone. And you, the owner, won't have to repeatedly answer the same "What am I supposed to do?" question.

YOUR BUSINESS NAME

This is an area that I almost really screwed up when I created my former spa. Fortunately, I got some great advice which I will pass along to you.

I spent months trying to figure out what to name my esthetics business. I scribbled things down, I drew logos, and I asked everyone I knew for their opinion. I spent a lot of time on it and had some fabulous names. I have to admit, it was a lot of fun. But then I got some wonderful advice which was: <u>Your business name needs to tell everybody exactly what you do</u>. That changed everything for me.

My business name ended up being "Skin Renewal Center."

As I have said previously, back then in the year 2000, everyone was a "day spa." Although I considered myself a day spa, and originally planned to use "day spa" in the name, ultimately I did not use the word "spa" in any form. And I am so glad I did not.

Another reason for not limiting yourself by using "spa" or "day spa" in your business name is that if you ever decide you want to transform into a hair removal only business, or a clinical facial specialty, your business name would no longer fit.

I didn't love the name "Skin Renewal Center" at first because I thought it was too boring and bland. But as it turned out, it was the perfect name. It very clearly described what we did. It contained the crucial word "skin" which was the primary nature of my esthetics business. "Renewal" is a positive word and very clearly answers the "What's in it for me?" question, which we know is what the client is thinking.

The word "skin" being the first word in the name "Skin Renewal Center" was important for a few reasons. It is an easy word to remember and to spell and is really closely associated with esthetics. So if a prospective client could remember nothing else, they would be able to find us online (or in the phone book back then) by simply searching for "skin" in the city in which we were located. Of course, these days there are lots of esthetics business that contain the word "skin" however, with a bit of scrolling down the page, they could find us. It is certainly easier than trying to remember and find a person's first name or a generic word.

The font. I wanted the font to be fancy and unique. However, I got another piece of great advice which was that the signage must be easy to read from afar, such as when people are driving by or walking by. It also must be dark writing on a light background, or vice versa.

A new development that we must consider today is that school children are not necessarily learning cursive writing anymore. And those kids will grow up to be your esthetics clients someday so be certain to use a font that everybody can read...forever.

Décor and ambience. This is very personal to you, so you can do whatever you want to do, of course. However, there are some studies which you may find helpful about how certain music and specific colors can influence people's behavior.

With the right music and color choices, people will stay longer, buy more, and feel better while they are in your space. Therefore, you may want to do a little research before choosing wall paint, or carpet colors, etc.

Certain scents will wake people up and invigorate them, and others will calm and relax them. Because scents are an element of our work, it is crucial to determine which scents to use and when to use them.

BEHIND THE SCENES: A Note to Spa Owners

A common fear is that Estheticians might someday want to leave your spa and take clients with them. While this is a legitimate concern, it is not an insurmountable one. Spa owners and managers must independently make an effort to create a solid bond between the client and the spa. This is your best shot at ensuring that the client will choose to stay with the spa even if the Esthetician is no longer there.

The best way for a spa to create that loyal bond is simply to show the clients they care. This starts with stellar customer service offered by the owner, manager, front desk staff and all other employees whom the clients will encounter before and after they step into the treatment room.

Other important factors are the location of the spa, easy parking, convenient hours of operation and personal service whenever possible. Additionally, very often, the spa can afford to offer additional perks that another spa or Solo Esthetician cannot, so keep that in mind and use it to your advantage.

OWNERSHIP and MANAGEMENT

When I was attending my esthetics program so many years ago, we would talk amongst ourselves about what sort of job we wanted and how much we expected to be paid. Some of us (like me) dreamed of having our own place. However, after being an Esthetician for a couple of decades, owning a spa, and being a Solo Esthetician, I came to have an entirely different perspective. So, for any of you who may be newly licensed, I want to offer my thoughts about why you should consider going to work for somebody else before you go out on your own.

I am going to begin with my day spa which I started right out of esthetics school because I expect some of you are thinking of doing the same thing.

SKIN RENEWAL CENTER

I will tell you about my experience with opening a spa soon after earning my Esthetician license. I do not necessarily recommend you do it that way, but I will tell you how it went for me in the hopes that you will find something in my story that will be helpful to you.

My dream ("Plan A"): The short version of "how it all began" is that I left a successful career as a court reporter and followed a distant dream to create a wellness center for women...even though I had no idea how to make that happen. Obviously, it is quite a leap to go from an environment of angry lawyers and contentious lawsuits to a peaceful, tranquil spa environment where everyone is happy.

My original intent was to open a small starter spa before moving on to a larger facility. The plan was that I would be the Solo Esthetician until it got busy enough that I could afford to hire another

Esthetician to replace me in the treatment room. However, things did not turn out that way.

Even though my long range goal did not include working in the treatment room, I was well aware back then that I did not know how to build and manage a wellness center. And I also knew that I needed to start small so I could keep it affordable and easy to manage. So my first step was to enroll in an Esthetician licensing program in my area, which I did shortly after my son went off to kindergarten. I knew I had to learn everything I could about this business, from how to give a facial to how to use a cash register.

Shortly after earning my Esthetician license, I signed myself up for a Spa Director's intensive, week-long, full-time, in-person course. It was there I learned the business side of owning a day spa. I also took esthetics classes beyond what I learned in my esthetics program because I knew I had not learned enough there. Admittedly I came into this new career fully aware that I was not sufficiently prepared, and that's okay because it created a determination in me to get prepared.

A few months later, I leased a space in a small shopping center and transformed it into my day spa. There was a lot of construction along the way which resulted in a few snags with the permit process but in 2000, Skin Renewal Center opened her doors.

My spa. I had 700 square feet which started out as one facial room, one massage room, and the third was a spray tan room. Eventually, the spray tan room became a second facial room.

I also had a front desk, laundry area, waiting room and a retail area with a makeup bar where we offered custom-blended makeup.

My staff. My spa was located in a college town so all of my front desk employees were college students. There were the occasional ups and downs of college life, but we really did become one big happy family and we made some wonderful memories together.

My reality ("Plan B"). As far as my original plan which was to stay only briefly in the treatment room, well, the reason that didn't happen as planned is because I fell in love with esthetics and my clients. In fact, I ended up working happily in the treatment room for 15 years.

Eventually, I sold that spa to an employee when my family relocated about 40 miles away. Since then, my spa has been sold a couple more times and last I heard, it is still going strong which makes me very happy. In my new city, I opened a solo esthetics practice. Although I did not solicit any of my former spa clients, many of them followed me when I relocated and actually drove quite a distance to do so. What an honor.

My lessons. Earning an Esthetician license, in my opinion, is akin to receiving the key that unlocks the door to the field of esthetics. By that I mean, having your license is only the first step in becoming a financially successful Esthetician.

Some esthetics programs do teach their students well beyond license exam preparation, but it is a mistake to assume that your esthetics program will be enough to propel you directly to the successful esthetics career that you are dreaming of. Being an Esthetician is not just about facials and skin care. It is a business. Therefore, you must take it upon yourself to seek education that will prepare you for the business of esthetics.

BEHIND THE SCENES: A Note to New Estheticians

My advice. Probably the most important piece of advice I would give to new Estheticians is this:

When you are in school and are planning your future esthetics career, you may think that you should get a job that looks a certain way and pays a certain amount. My suggestion is that you do not get too caught up in that stuff.

If you get a job where you are paid a lot but don't learn anything or the spa owner doesn't really know what he or she is doing, your career path will be delayed. Precious time will be lost between starting out and reaching your ultimate goals. Looking back over the last 20 years of my esthetics career, which includes being a Spa Owner and a Solo Esthetician, I would have done things differently. I wish someone would have given to me the advice back then that I am giving to you right now.

Although many of today's esthetics licensing programs are fabulous (certainly compared to the training I got in 1999), your esthetics school really has only one requirement which is to prepare you to pass your licensing exam. It is impossible for the school to prepare you for every conceivable job or task you may encounter, due to the fact that esthetics changes all the time.

Secondly, employers may not (in fact, usually don't) have a training program in place to prepare you for the real world of esthetics. For this reason, it is essential that new Estheticians take as many classes outside of their esthetics program as possible.

Thirdly, do not expect your first job to be your dream job. In fact, don't even look for a "dream job." Instead, seek out a first job which offers you the opportunity to learn the most.

When you begin your esthetics career working for someone else, you will be exposed to many things that will help you when the time comes that you are ready to go out on your own. For example, you will learn how Estheticians are paid, how schedules are set, what perks might be available for employees. You learn a lot about the management side of the esthetics business as you watch how your employer does it, which will likely also expose you to management styles that you do not like. Keep in mind, sometimes the best lessons are about what <u>not</u> to do.

Best of all, if you work for somebody else, you can make your newbie mistakes on somebody else's clients which is a heck of a lot better than making them on your own clients. Your first few facials in the treatment room might not be your best, so think like an athlete and practice, practice, practice. Practice your moves on your friends, your family, and even your pets! For obvious reasons, this is so much better than making those first newbie mistakes on your own clients.

HIRING ESTHETICIANS

At some point, if and when you go out on your own, you might need to hire employees, so I am going to tell you about my hiring process. I will provide you with some interview questions you are free to use.

Basically, my process was to have interested candidates submit a resume to me and if I was interested in the resume, I would invite them in for an in-person verbal interview. If they impressed me during that interview, the next step would be a practical interview.

Estheticians need to know how to perform esthetics services, of course; however, in my opinion, other things are far more important. An Esthetician can continue to learn to improve his or her esthetics skills. However, people skills, their personality, and a team player attitude...those are inherent in a person, and I learned rather quickly these traits are primarily what I needed to look for. Oh, I tried it the traditional way, relying exclusively on the resume, but I quickly realized the resume method was much less dependable.

Below are interview questions that I developed with which to assess potential candidates. When you look at these questions, it is important to understand that there are no right and wrong answers. They are not the old school sort of interview questions, so candidates will not necessarily be prepared to answer them. That means you will catch them a little off guard which will result in gaining a bit more insight into their character.

Lastly, do not be afraid to rely at least somewhat on your intuition. It is your internal GPS system. Use it!

Interview Questions

1. Name and date licensed
2. Do you have any post-graduate training: Which classes? How recently?

3. Have you attended any esthetics trade shows? Which ones? How recently? How often?
4. What made you decide to become an Esthetician?
5. What is your favorite part of being an Esthetician?
6. What is your least favorite part of being an Esthetician?
7. Which esthetics services have you had the most experience in?
8. What do you think you are best at?
9. Describe your favorite type of client?
10. Describe your least favorite type of client?
11. Which skin care lines are you familiar with?
12. Tell me about a bad experience you've had at work? How did you handle it?
13. Have you had any personality conflicts with co-workers? How did you handle it?
14. Have you had any personality conflicts with employers? How did you handle it?
15. What experience, if any, have you had with providing customer service?
16. Have you ever built up a client base? How did you do it? How many clients did you have?
17. Have you ever worked on commission (service and/or retail)?
18. How comfortable are you with retail sales? How do you see it as part of your esthetics work?
19. What would be your 3 most important contributions to (name of your business) and its clients?
20. What are your future goals: How long do you intend to remain in the esthetics business?
21. Any limitations on your work schedule? Nights? Weekends?
22. How many hours are you currently available to work per week? Any plans for that to change?
23. Do you have any particular responsibilities or commitments that would conflict with your work schedule?
24. Do you understand the difference between working at a spa/resort with transient clients, and working at (name of your business)?

As you read through these interview questions, keep in mind that your primary goal is to determine if this person is a team player. You are assessing their attitude, their general demeanor, their passion for esthetics. And you are also trying to figure out if they are going to be a good fit for your esthetics business.

I want to point out one specific question on this page which is number 20 "future plans." The reason this question matters is because if they tell you they plan to have their own spa someday, you then have to decide if they are worth the risk. Do you want to the spend the time and money involved in hiring them, training them for a year or two, and then having them open their own esthetics business someday to complete with you? (Sometimes the answer is yes, it is worth the risk.)

Post Interview Notes. Immediately after the interview, be sure to make notes about everything you can think of because if you are going through a lot of candidates, it will become a blur. This is the outline I used for my notes:

- Appearance
- Communication skills
- Enthusiasm
- Second interview: yes/no
- Practical skills
- Background check: (full name, driver's license and address)
- References from last employer or esthetics program

BEHIND THE SCENES: A Note to Spa Owners

When it comes to hiring Estheticians, it is always an advantage when whomever is assessing the candidates is also licensed Esthetician. But if that is not your situation, at least include your most-trusted Esthetician somewhere in the hiring process or bring in a qualified consultant who is an Esthetician to help you.

Estheticians can spot things that a non-Esthetician cannot. For example, the most esthetically skilled or experienced candidate is not always the best candidate. You want a team player, a good fit for your business and someone whose personality will represent your brand well.

Because the goal of most esthetics programs is simply to prepare the students to pass the state licensing exam, this means it is possible that the best fit for your business may be someone who needs extra training. Skills can be learned, but personality, good energy and dependability are already there....or they're not.

My advice is to look for Estheticians who have availed themselves of post-graduate training on their own. Meet the best candidates in person and use your instincts to assess whether they are a good fit for your business. Do not be afraid to hire a newly-licensed Esthetician. Sometimes the old-timers who have many years under their belt have not kept up with the rapidly evolving field of esthetics, and a newbie might very well be the better choice.

RETAIL ROCKS!

When it comes to retail, our main goal is to provide clients with education and guidance about skin care products and protocols that will provide optimal skin health. It is not our job to try to talk people into buying something, so I am not going to give you various methods with which to sell. Instead, we must make access to our products easy for shoppers.

Clients' habits have been studied and analyzed, and there are a few helpful facts you should know. There is a specific science behind why people buy, and in this section I will give you documented info about how best to maximize your retail area.

SHOPPER BEHAVIOR

Initiating Contact. Give the client a chance to breathe before presenting her with questions about why she has come in. A friendly "hello" will suffice until she has had a chance to survey the area and hone in on whatever it is she may be interested in. Once she has done that, then it's okay to inquire how you might help her.

Decompression Zone. When it comes to shopper behavior, it's predictable in most cases. It starts with what I call "The Decompression Zone" which is typically the first 10 feet a customer encounters as they enter a space. If your business is small, 10 feet could be halfway into the treatment room. But basically, people just need a moment to take in what they are looking at, breathe a little bit, and feel comfortable.

Of course, give them a friendly greeting, but it's not wise to immediately go into the "Here's all our specials, here's what's on sale, let me know if you need anything." Rather, just give them a second. It's kind of like when you are online and you search for a website you want to view but before you have even briefly scanned the page to see if you're interested, an opt-in box pops up asking you to sign up for their emails. It's just so annoying. So, let's not be annoying to people who enter our business.

No "yes" or "no." It's also important not to ask "yes" or "no" questions such as "May I help you?" because that calls for a simple "yes" or "no" answer. If they have not decompressed yet, they will likely say "no" and that's the end of the conversation. If instead you say "What can I help you with today?" of course, they could say "nothing," but they could also say "Oh, I'm looking for...." In other words, you have better odds of getting a more detailed answer if you avoid a "yes" or "no" question, and you will be more equipped to help them with whatever it is they are interested in.

SIGNAGE

Prices. I am often asked whether prices should be visible on or near our retail products. My answer is a resounding YES! Definitely provide pricing so as to avoid sticker shock and to avoid forcing shoppers to ask about prices. Asking for the price makes a lot of people uncomfortable, therefore many people won't ask, and they won't buy.

Let shoppers decide for themselves privately whether the product is within their budget. It is embarrassing for a shopper to have to ask the price of something and then realize he or she can't afford it. We must avoid causing any discomfort to someone who has come into our business hoping to spend their money with us.

Eyesight. As I mentioned earlier, eyesight can be an issue for some people. It could be a lighting problem, the size of the font, or an ink choice...all of which may discourage a shopper from a purchase they would otherwise make.

For some people, it won't matter because they won't read the label anyway. However, statistics show that 91% of shoppers will read the front of the packaging, and 43% will turn it over and read the back. I suggest this is something you prepare for because if shoppers must reach into their purse or pocket to grab their reading glasses, they may just skip it and move on, and there goes a potential sale.

Butt Brush Factor: And the next one is the Butt Brush Factor which I think is pretty funny. This one applies mostly to women.

The Butt Brush Factor is when a woman is browsing in an area that is narrow, so much so that it feels to her that anybody who walks by them will touch her — specifically butts would brush up against each other. If she feel that possibility exists (even if it actually does not), a woman will not stay in that area very long. She will move out of the way and therefore won't buy whatever it is you are promoting or displaying in that area.

Samples. More than ever, shoppers want to touch and smell products. The good news about this is that once a client has interacted with a product, there becomes an element of ownership with that item. So, if you provide shoppers with that opportunity, your retail sales will rise.

Be aware that handing out samples is not a substitute for selling retail products. It is essential that samples are only offered as part of a detailed discussion between the Esthetician and the customer.

The most common and easiest way to encourage a shopper's interaction with products is by sampling, such as:

- Sample bar – This is like a toy box for adults. They are able to interact with many products at once, try them on, compare them and bond with them.
- Companies are not offering free samples to Estheticians as often as they used to, but even if you have to purchase samples, it is a good investment in future retail sales for all of the reasons given above.
- Sampling dramatically reduces and/or completely eliminates return of products. This reason alone is worth the minimal extra expense of providing samples.

RETAIL

Displays. Research shows that the best-selling location on retail shelves is at bulls-eye level. The next best-selling location is just slightly right of that. So put items that you really want to sell at the bullseye area or slightly to the right.

It is important to move your products around regularly, in sync with your regularly scheduled appointments. If most of your clients come in every 4 to 6 weeks for a service, then every 4-6 weeks is when you should modify your retail area somewhat, either by rearranging the products on the shelf or by changing the decorations. Even a minor tweaking will make a big difference.

Artsy displays. Also determined from research into what compels people to buy is that shoppers are hesitant to disturb an "artsy" display. Meaning if a product they want to purchase is part of a dramatic display, they won't touch it. If it's too cute, too artsy, too perfectly stacked on each other, or balanced on top of something, clients will hesitate to disturb the display. So keep this in mind, and always err on the side of making it easy for customers to buy.

One way to avoid this problem is to be sure there are singular products in front of your artsy displays so customers can grab a product without messing up your work of art.

The Last Product. The same thing goes for the last product on the shelf. Clients will hesitate to take the last product so at the very least, if you don't have a lot of product in stock, use some of the product's empty packaging to place on your shelf so the shelf looks full even though half of them are empty boxes.

Borrow from the pros. When you are trying to get creative with your retail area, don't forget that big department stores put a lot of money into hiring professionals to design their displays. So follow their lead because they have done the homework for you! Visit your favorite high-end stores to get some ideas and snap a few photos. Then you can rework those ideas to fit your business.

THE SHOPPING EXPERIENCE

Make it Easy. Your client's shopping experience should have some thought put into it. You must make it easy for people to buy from you. Sounds elementary, I know, yet unfortunately, rarely do businesses take this into consideration and plan ahead.

M.Y.O.B. Mind your own business. Don't ever assume how much money a client can or cannot afford to spend. It is none of your business!

Credit Cards. Obviously, you must take credit cards....all of them. We don't want to tell clients how to spend their money or restrict the method by which they choose to pay us. I am baffled by those who refuse to accept American Express due to the minimal extra transaction charge. Why would you not want American Express card holders to buy from you? American Express offers some great perks for cardholders, so of course they would prefer to use that card. So why force a client to use a different card?

Girl Friends. It is a studied and proven fact that women will spend more money when they are shopping with their BFFs. That is really good news for us because we can easily use that factoid to our benefit by holding regular events for women at our place of business.

Hands Free. Clients will only purchase as much as they can hold, which means when their hands are full, they will stop shopping. When you consider that women will likely have a purse in one hand, it means they will be limited to only the other hand for shopping.

The solution for this is either to keep an eye out for a shopper's hands becoming full and offer to hold her products at the front desk, or have shopping bags or baskets readily available for her use.

More is More. The more time a shopper spends in your retail area, the more money he or she will spend. Make it a pleasant experience with lots of products to sample, literature to read, and assistance with packages.

No-Fault Return Policy. Unless you have a problematic client who makes a habit of using and returning products, just go ahead and take it back. If it's one of your regular clients, do it with a big smile and no questions asked. That goodwill gesture is worth a lot more in client loyalty and future purchases than you may have lost with the occasional returned product which might be outside your posted return policy date.

Free Shipping. We must make it easy and painless for clients to replenish their products so that they aren't tempted to buy online or at another store. Free shipping is a great way to accomplish that.

Here is how I did it without losing any money:

I raised the price of my retail products an additional 25 cents, and that extra profit went into my theoretical "shipping fund." On the occasions I need to ship products, I am compensated by my shipping fund. Because I do not ship very often, most of the shipping fund went unused which allowed me to spend that portion on client gifts or client events.

You don't have to see the whole staircase.
Just take the first step.
~Martin Luther King, Jr.

9 LEGAL ISSUES

LIABILITY INSURANCE

It is essential that Estheticians have liability insurance, and here's why: Consumers have a right to expect that the Esthetician offering a service is qualified to safely perform that service. In other words, consumers have a legal right not to be harmed. However, as we know, even the best-trained and most-qualified Estheticians can make a mistake. Unexpected things happen, equipment fails…and we must protect ourselves. That is what liability insurance is for.

I hear the term "sue happy" thrown about by Estheticians frequently. I am here to tell you: That is absolute nonsense. This term is typically used as an excuse by an Esthetician who has not been doing things properly. Yes, there are a lot of lawsuits in this country, and, yes, some of them are frivolous. However, there is no blaming the client when he or she has been hurt.

It is frightening how many Estheticians do not understand the necessity of having their own liability insurance. Often technicians employed by spas or esthetics businesses assume they are covered by their employer's insurance. But how many of those Estheticians have actually read their employer's insurance policy and are 100% clear on exactly what is covered?

Even if the Esthetician has read the policy, and understands it, how can he or she be certain the insurance premiums are being paid in a timely manner by their employer? If the payments are delinquent, the policy will be cancelled, and that means nobody is covered.

Liability insurance for Estheticians is affordable and worth every penny.

As the field of esthetics becomes more clinical and high-tech, it is a mistake to assume that everything we are tempted to purchase and use on clients will be covered by our liability insurance.

You should always know specifically what is covered by your own liability policy before you purchase the latest and coolest new piece of esthetic equipment. You might be really surprised to learn what is not covered. For example, not all electrical equipment is covered, and there are some services that are commonly excluded.

If you are not 100% certain whether something is covered, call your insurance company and get it clarified. Do not rely on advice you receive on social media.

You should also verify what you can and cannot do under your Esthetician license. If something goes wrong and you find that you are not covered by insurance and/or you are operating outside the rules of your Esthetician license, you are in very big trouble, legally and financially. Do not let that happen.

CONSENT FORMS

There is a misunderstanding among Estheticians regarding the purpose of a Consent Form, so let's set that straight right now.

A consent form will not absolve you of liability if you have actually done something wrong which resulted in a client being harmed. What a Consent Form will do is serve as evidence that you explained to the client the service, the procedure, any contraindications, and the expected results. The client's signature on the document serves as evidence that they understood.

I suggest you create your own Consent Forms to fit your particular esthetics business. It is essential that clients sign a new Consent Form every time they begin a new service. For example, if they usually have facials but now they will be having a peel, a "peel consent form" should be signed. Do whatever fits the situation but when in doubt, err on the side of caution.

Do not over-promise results. The Esthetician must be honest about what the client can expect. Above all, do not be afraid to say NO to something that your instincts tell you is not right. For example, if you suspect a client has recently been in a tanning booth, decline or delay the aggressive peel they may be requesting.

If something goes wrong and you have no consent form and therefore no proof that the client was made aware of possible contraindications before the service was performed, you are putting your client's health and your Esthetician license (and possibly your entire career) at risk.

Consent forms are simple and important. Use them.

LICENSING

It goes without saying that anyone who holds a license issued by their state must know the laws and rules that govern that license. However, it is far too common among Estheticians that either they do not realize how important it is to know those laws and rules, or they just don't care.

We are in a profession where we can (and sometimes do) harm people. When that happens, the standards and reputation of the Esthetician drops immeasurably. You must know the scope of your license, what services you are allowed to perform, and what equipment you are allowed to use.

Keeping informed. I constantly hear Estheticians complain that their state board does not inform them of changes in laws and new rules that may be pending. However, please understand, it is not the licensing board's responsibility to babysit us. We are licensed professionals, and it is our job to keep ourselves informed.

Most of us spend plenty of time online, so it is easy to follow our state licensing board on social media, or simply do a quick internet search occasionally to check for pending legislation. At the very least, when it is time to renew your Esthetician license, look through your state licensing board's website and see if anything has changed since you last renewed.

State Board meetings. You can attend your state board meetings in person, and in some states, the meeting is available via livestream. In my experience, having attended many California board meetings, I can tell you that there are usually very few Estheticians in attendance. This means that when something controversial is presented to the board at an official meeting, there are no Estheticians in the audience to clarify any misinformation the board may have been given.

Perhaps you are under the impression that your board is made up entirely of Estheticians, but that is not necessarily the case. Therefore, we need Estheticians who are currently working in the treatment room to help protect our profession by attending state board meetings and speaking up.

If Estheticians are not going to be actively involved, then they really can't complain if things don't go the way they want them to. In my state, the board's agenda is posted online well in advance of the meeting. Anyone can see what is coming up, and they get involved. There is always a call for public comments before anything is passed or any rules are changed; however, rarely do Estheticians take this important opportunity to show up and speak to the board.

It is only when a rule has been changed or a privilege has been taken away from us, that Estheticians show up. At that point, Estheticians typically show up in large numbers, mad as heck, accusing the licensing board of taking away their livelihood and not wanting them to make money. However, most of the time, the accusations Estheticians bring to the board meeting are incorrect (probably because they got their information from social media).

Legislation. When it comes to legislation that will impact Estheticians, always go directly to the source for info. Do not rely on social media. One of the best pieces of advice I ever got was "Look under the hood of the car" which means just because something looks shiny and pretty and sounds good at first glance, do not assume it is good for YOU.

The hood of the car. I know of states that want to implement various other esthetics-related licenses. For example, Master Esthetician. Sounds good, I know. But look under the hood of the car. Who is sponsoring this bill? Is it perhaps a school owner who will benefit financially if we ALL must go back to school to achieve this elevated license?

And if we do go back to school to achieve this elevated license, are the advantages enormous? Or are they few, and not enough to entice an employer to pay the extra money to hire someone with this license?

Consider who is qualified to apply for this elevated license? Only those who have completed the Esthetician training hours that are currently required? Or does it also include cosmetologists who have had only a few hours of official esthetics training?

Look under the hood of the car and ask, "What's in it for me?" before being lured by a fancy title that might cost a lot of money and in the long run, may not be of any real financial (or other) benefit.

EMPLOYEE v. IC

Am I an employee or an Independent Contractor?

When it comes to whether an Esthetician is an employee or an IC, it can be really confusing both for the Esthetician and for the employer. But as a business owner who might someday hire staff or other Estheticians, it is important that you know the difference between these two classifications.

A business may pay an Independent Contractor and an employee for the same or similar work, but there are important legal differences between the two.

The overall difference is simply who calls the shots and makes the decisions. If the individual is an employee, then the employer will make the decisions and the employee is required to follow the employer's rules. Whereas an Independent Contractor is considered self-employed and therefore they make their own decisions. For Estheticians, this may include decisions regarding which products to use and sell, which services to offer, which days/hours to work.

TAXES

Employee. For the employee, the company withholds income tax, Social Security, and Medicare from wages paid. If you are an owner and this sounds like an insurmountable obstacle for you, look into payroll companies because you may discover that the money you spend hiring a payroll company to do your weekly or monthly payroll and taxes makes more financial sense than doing it yourself.

Typically, you will make more money working in your treatment room than you will pay out to a payroll company. This is what I did when I had my spa, and it might be something you should investigate. The advantage of using a payroll company is that you know they are doing it correctly and in a timely manner. You do not have to stress out about it; instead, you can stay in your treatment room and make lots of money doing what you love to do.

Independent Contractor. The employer does not withhold taxes which means the Independent Contractor is responsible for paying federal and state taxes on their own. Employment and labor laws also do not apply to Independent Contractors.

Consequences of Treating an Employee as an Independent Contractor. The IRS encourages all businesses and business owners to know the rules when it comes to classifying a worker as an employee or an Independent Contractor.

If you classify an employee as an Independent Contractor and you have no reasonable basis for doing so, you may be held liable for employment taxes for that worker. (See Internal Revenue Code section 3509 for more information.)

An employer must withhold income taxes and pay Social Security, Medicare taxes and unemployment tax on wages paid to an employee. Employers normally do not have to withhold or pay any taxes on payments to Independent Contractors.

The information that follows is copied from the IRS website "Independent Contractor (Self-Employed) or Employee":

Classifying workers:

Here are two key points for small business owners to keep in mind when it comes to classifying workers:

Control. The relationship between a worker and a business is important. If the business controls what work is accomplished and directs how it is done, it exerts behavioral control. If the business directs or controls financial and certain relevant aspects of a worker's job, it exercises financial control. This includes:

- The extent of the worker's investment in the facilities or tools used in performing services

- The extent to which the worker makes his or her services available to the relevant market
- How the business pays the worker, and
- The extent to which the worker can realize a profit or incur a loss

Relationship. How the employer and worker perceive their relationship is also important for determining worker status. Key topics to think about include:

- Written contracts describing the relationship the parties intended to create
- Whether the business provides the worker with employee-type benefits, such as insurance, a pension plan, vacation, or sick pay
- The permanency of the relationship
- The extent to which services performed by the worker are a key aspect of the regular business of the company
- The extent to which the worker has unreimbursed business expenses

National Coalition of Esthetics Association (NCEA)

NCEA's primary mission is to help Estheticians protect their career and earning potential, and has been doing so since 2000. Once you become a member of NCEA, you can work towards getting your National Esthetician Certification so you know you have met the equivalent standards of a Master Esthetician.

Although a state Master Esthetician license is currently available in only 4 states (UT, VA, DC, WA), getting the NCEA Certified credential shows that you have voluntarily raised your competency to the same level. We need to show legislators that this is the licensing level we want to be in order to change our future. *(Excerpted from the NCEA website)*

NCEA CERTIFIED

I have been NCEA Certified since 2008 and I am very proud of this certification. In case you are not familiar with NCEA Certification, it is the national certification for Estheticians and is equivalent to the level of Master Esthetician.

My California Esthetician licensing required only 600 hours of training which may have made sense back in 1999 when I earned my Esthetician license, but it does not make sense now. Nor does it make sense that we have no continuing education requirements in my state, especially considering how clinical today's esthetics has become.

However, as an NCEA Certified Esthetician, I must complete 12 units of Continuing Education every 3 years, as well as re-certify in CPR/AED/First Aid. I must also submit proof of a current Esthetician license, and proof of liability insurance.

I am very proud to be an NCEA Certified Professional Esthetician and over the years, I have participated with NCEA and NCEA Certified events in various ways and in various places. I have hosted the NETT Conference (National Esthetic Teachers Training), I have been an NCEA trainer and have led NCEA Certification preparedness classes for those who prefer a class setting rather than studying solo. And in 2019, I became one of the first few to receive the Lifetime NCEA Certification.

You can find more info on the NCEA Certified website: www.ncea.tv

You've always had the power, my dear.
You just had to learn it for yourself.
~Glinda the Good Witch

10 **NETWORKING**

Well, I've saved the fun stuff for the last chapter. Here we will discuss networking with other Estheticians, attending trade shows, hanging out with the people who understand our language and share our never-ending interest in talking about skin care. We need these people in our lives because it is good for our soul and for our sanity.

Sometimes we get so ensconced in our treatment rooms that we lose touch with what is going on in the world of esthetics. That is how we get stuck in a rut and become stale…and that can paralyze an otherwise promising career in esthetics.

If you cannot get out of your treatment room, there are fabulous trade magazines available that you can read in hard copy or online. These authors and educators have done the work for us, all we have to do is read and learn!

Social Media. With the advent of the internet came online message boards also known these days as communities. There you can get questions answered, learn about new ingredients and equipment, and find information about upcoming trade shows and educational opportunities – all without ever leaving your treatment room.

If you are a seasoned Esthetician, you know that we are only as strong as our weakest link. Mentoring an Esthetician who is coming up the ranks behind you helps us all.

One serious warning though: When participating in online message boards, be absolutely certain that you qualify your advisors. By this I mean, question their expertise. Hidden behind their computers, people unabashedly offer information and advice that they may not be qualified to give. So do ask! Ask for their credentials and experience on the topic for which they are offering advice. Especially if your money will be involved.

Do not fall prey to the "negative know-it-alls" who frequent free online message boards. They have nothing invested in the outcome, which typically means those who are struggling or failing will always be the loudest and most talkative on these boards.

Having an Esthetician license is not enough to qualify somebody as an expert, so beware. It is much like shopping for jeans; try the advice on and see how it fits you. If it doesn't fit, put it down and walk away.

TRADE SHOWS

I love a trade show for so many reasons. Just as our clients bond with our products once they have experienced them by smelling them, touching them, applying them, we should do the same. That is the only way we can relate to what our client's experience will be with a product. We must preview everything. We must try it on. We must see if we like it and see if it works.

At a trade show, licensed Estheticians can usually purchase a single product rather than being forced to meet the company's usual minimum order requirement. That's because it behooves the vendor to have Estheticians sample their products and take items back to our treatment room to try with our clients. That is the only true way to know whether the company's products are something we want to bring into our esthetics business.

Trade shows offer so many educational opportunities for very little cost, and they are held throughout the country and the world. If you find yourself stuck in a rut, one trade show will change everything for you. In all these years, I have never walked away from a trade show without being excited by at least one thing I learned, and I am always so glad that I attended.

We are lucky to be in a career that can go on for decades. It will change and evolve, and we must do the same.

RECIPE FOR SUCCESS

Another corny analogy: Your esthetics business is like a pie. You get to choose each ingredient as if you were going to add it to your pie. Just as the ingredients you choose for your pie will make it different from another's pie, the ingredients you choose for your esthetics business is what will make your esthetics business specific to YOU.

The best place to assess and select the ingredients for your esthetics business is at a trade show. Each vendor booth offers different ingredients. You get to smell, touch, and collect info about the ingredients before you decide whether to add it to your recipe. A trade show is like a one-stop shopping area for your esthetics business.

Here is a list of various things you can find at a trade show. Obviously, there is much more than what I have included here, but if you have not yet attended a professional trade show for Estheticians, this will give you an idea of what you might find.

- Products
- Services
- Demos
- Samples
- Equipment
- Tools
- Supplies
- Packaging
- Furniture

- Publications
- Music
- Software

EDUCATION AND EXPOSURE

Education: There are so many educational resources at a trade show. There are new things for you to learn and info you can take back with you to share with your clients. You can experience demos of all sorts of things, you can play with equipment, and you can experiment with products.

To me, a trade show is Esthetician nirvana. You can probably imagine how many times I have been on the verge of burnout over the 20+ years I have been an Esthetician. But all it takes for me is a couple of days at a tradeshow and I am reinvigorated…every time.

One of my favorite parts of a trade show is getting together with my Esthetician friends and hearing what they have discovered on the vendor floor, and then I can go check it out for myself. It is like having an advance team who scouts the area and points me to the good stuff!

GETTING THE MOST OUT OF A TRADE SHOW

I've learned a lot about trade shows since I have been to so many, in so many places, over so many years. I've been a speaker, an attendee and a Master of Ceremonies, so I have seen it from different perspectives. And there are a few things I'd like to share with you, especially for those of you who may not be familiar with these events yet.

First of all, these are international shows which means that vendors will be exhibiting from all over the country and the world. You must keep in mind that just because a vendor is exhibiting in a certain state does not mean their product or piece of equipment is legal for you to use in your state.

Obviously, the vendors are there to sell you something, and it is not their job to know what is legal in all 50 states. Therefore, do not rely on advice they may give you without first confirming with your own state board.

I suggest planning ahead if you are going to attend a trade show, and here's why: You will get the best rate on tickets, hotels and flights, and you won't have to wait in the long lines that are unavoidable the day of the show.

By planning in advance, you can snag a room at one of the hotels that are within walking distance to the convention center. That is especially handy for dropping off your purchases throughout the day, which frees up your hands for more shopping.

Another advantage is that if you need to get away from the action for a bit, you'll be able to sneak to your hotel room for a nap or a snack, or to change shoes, or whatever. At the end of the day when it's time to get together with the gang at a restaurant, you won't have all your trade show goodies to lug around with you.

Many vendors offer show specials, which means you can get things at discounted prices that you are able to take home with you. This is especially good if you just want to buy a couple of items to take back to your treatment room and play with before deciding whether to place an official order. If you happen to be around in the afternoon on the last day of the show, oftentimes vendors will dramatically drop their prices so that they won't have to schlep their wares back with them when the show closes.

Rolling bags. I must mention rolling bags because it is a pet peeve of mine. I do not actually remember when these weapons came on the scene at trade shows, but they cause a lot of trouble and a lot of injuries. Perhaps you are not aware that there is usually a very safe and secure "package check" at the event where you can safely drop off your purchases and your rolling bags.

NAVIGATING A TRADE SHOW

Navigation: I want to begin this section by telling you the story of my first trade show. I don't remember which one it was…I think maybe it was Las Vegas, which is an enormous show. I was still in Esthetician school and a bunch of us went to the show together.

Talk about overwhelming! It was definitely fun but I did the worst thing you can do, which is what we all do when we don't know any better. We just wandered down each aisle as a group, taking it all in and stopping at every vendor booth we encountered.

We really didn't know anything about the vendors other than we recognized the skin care line we were using in our Esthetician program. We excitedly collected everything each vendor gave us and tossed it into that enormous bag given to everyone by the sponsoring vendor as we entered the show.

Later I went back to my hotel room, and I dumped the contents of the very big bag onto my bed. I felt like a kid on Halloween! But that feeling faded quickly when I realized that the samples and the accompanying literature were not attached to each other. Therefore, nothing made sense to me.

The fact that I was so tired, so overwhelmed, and so confused hit me hard …and I broke into tears. In that moment, I was convinced that I was probably not going to make it through Esthetician school, I would never get my Esthetician license, and even if I did, I probably would be a lousy Esthetician. OMG, that's so funny now considering how far I have come in my esthetics career, but trust me….it was not funny back then!

So the moral of that story is: If you have moments in your career when you think you are not going to make it, you will. Just hang in there!

Eventually I figured out a better way to navigate a trade show and avoid this problem in the future. Of course, there are lots of ways to navigate a trade show, but I will tell you about my system just in case you'd like to borrow it until you figure out your own.

My system: First of all, I suggest you buy your tickets early so you will receive the show program prior to the show. Event programs vary, but generally you will find two important things inside the program: One is a complete list of exhibitors in alphabetical order which includes the booth number where they will be located in the exhibit hall.

The other is a diagram of the exhibit hall which includes all the booth numbers. (For purposes of this explanation, I will refer to these items as "List of Exhibitors" and "Diagram of Exhibit Hall" but they are often referred to by other terms.)

1. A complete **List of Exhibitors** with their booth numbers, presented in alphabetical order.
2. A **Diagram of Exhibit Hall** which gives the exhibit hall booth numbers, presented in alphabetical order.

The steps:

Make your own list of "priority vendors" which means anyone you absolutely must see. Maybe you need to purchase supplies, or renew your liability insurance, maybe you want to talk to a vendor about something, or perhaps there is a new product you have heard about and want to check out.

- In the show program, go to the **List of Exhibitors** and put a check mark by any vendors who are on your priority list and circle their booth number.
- In the show program, go to the **Diagram of Exhibit Hall** and circle the booth numbers that correspond to the vendors you have check-marked on the List of Exhibitors.

When you are at the trade show, you will see very large signs overhead which indicate the aisle numbers. For example, over the first aisle might be a sign that says 100, the next aisle will be 200 and so on.

You can keep your Diagram of Exhibit Hall open and simply hit all your priorities in numerical order which will keep you from jumping around all over the exhibit hall. (That's the mistake that will wear you out!)

You can always refer back to the List of Exhibitors that you have check-marked if you want to know in advance which vendor is at which booth.

Once I have completed my priorities, I take my goodies back to my hotel room and free up my hands. And then I go back to the show, and I am free to wander the aisles and browse to my heart's (and feet's) content. If my brain or feet get tired, it won't matter so much because my priority tasks have already been completed.

I hope to see you at a trade show soon!

If you do what you love, you'll never work a day in your life.
~Marc Anthony

GRATITUDE

Services, equipment, products and Estheticians will come and go,
but the HEART of Esthetics will always be
the foundation for success in this business.

Well, we've come to the end of this book. I wrote the original "The Heart of Esthetics" book in 2013 and you have just completed the updated 2022 version. Wow, so much has changed! I hope you have enjoyed reading this book as much as I enjoyed creating it for you.

The Heart of Esthetics book was definitely a passion project for me. I am driven by the fact that too many Estheticians are absorbing bad information on social media and various other online sites which will waste their time and their money and eventually lead them down a path to failure. Kudos to you for looking in the right place for solid information which will ultimately pave the way to your success.

I have had many mentors through my esthetics career and my best advice is to be sure you too have not just one mentor, but many. And if my book has served as a catalyst to help you discover your passion for esthetics (or rediscover it, if it was lost), that makes me happy. I hope you take with you lots of ideas and inspiration as well as newly-gained self-awareness which has amplified your confidence in your abilities to create and maintain the esthetics career of your dreams.

I want to remind you that it's really important to get out of your treatment room (regularly!) and mix and mingle with other Estheticians. Take a class, attend a trade show, or simply choose a few Estheticians from your favorite social media group and invite them to come to your business or your treatment room just to hang out, talk about products, services, equipment, whatever. It's important to spend time – in person – with people who speak your language. It will help you refresh, reset, and remember why you love esthetics.

I think it's really important work that we do and I've loved every minute of it. I'm eternally grateful for all the wonderful Estheticians and other participants in the spa business that I've had the honor to meet throughout my esthetics journey. I wish you as much success and fun in your career as I have had in mine.

Loyal clients are a gift. Treat them well.

And be grateful.

ABOUT THE AUTHOR

Diane Buccola has been a licensed Esthetician in the state of California since 1999. In 2009 she received her NCEA Certification which is the national certification for Estheticians, and in 2019 she was awarded the "Lifetime" NCEA Certification.

Diane has been a spa owner and Solo Esthetician, and over her many years in the spa business has served as a consultant, trainer, and mentor for Estheticians and spas, as well as a trainer for NCEA Certified prep classes. She has served on the Advisory Board of Les Nouvelles Esthetiques & Spa magazine, and has been a speaker and Master of Ceremonies at the International Congress of Esthetics & Spa.

Diane has authored three books: "The Heart of Esthetics," "Estheticians are a Girl's Best Friend," and "Notes from Your Fairy Godmother." In 2019, Diane created two online courses, "The Heart of Esthetics" and "The Ultimate Guide for New Estheticians," and in 2020, she launched the "Esthetician Solutions" membership site.

You can find Diane on Facebook @ Happy Esthetician or online at spabizboard.com.

www.ingramcontent.com/pod-product-compliance
Lightning Source LLC
Chambersburg PA
CBHW071204210326
41597CB00016B/1666